The Whiz Kid of
Wall Street's
Investment Guide

The Whiz Kid of Wall Street's Investment Guide

How I Returned 34 Percent on My Portfolio, and You Can, Too

Matt Seto

with Steven Levingston

William Morrow and Company, Inc.
New York

Library of Congress Cataloging-in-Publication Data

Seto, Matt, 1977–
The whiz kid of Wall Street's investment guide: how I returned 34 percent on my portfolio, and you can, too / by Matt Seto with Steven Levingston.
p.   cm.
ISBN 0–688–14567–1
1. Investments.   2. Stocks.   3. Portfolio management.
I. Levingston, Steven.   II. Title.
HG4521.S456   1995
332.6—dc20   95–41595
CIP

Printed in the United States of America

First Edition

1 2 3 4 5 6 7 8 9 10

BOOK DESIGN BY ROGER GREINER

I'D LIKE TO DEDICATE THIS BOOK

to my family, friends, and everybody who has been good to me.
I'm greatly indebted to you.

—M.S.

TO SUE AND KATIE

—S.L.

Acknowledgments

First and foremost, I'd like to acknowledge and thank Steve Levingston and Doris Cooper.

I have tremendous gratitude and awe for Steve Levingston and the astonishing writing and organizational talent that he brought to this book.

Doris Cooper, my editor at William Morrow, first came up with the idea for this book. Her hard work and natural talent for the craft and business of editing made *The Whiz Kid of Wall Street's Investment Guide* really happen—with great success like nobody else would have been capable of.

I was lucky to have both Steve and Doris as top-flight professionals. They made my transition from money manager and high school newspaper columnist to author very easy and enjoyable. I am indebted heavily to both of them.

I'd also like to thank Lazlo Birinyi, Jr., and Birinyi Associates, who were very generous in creating graphs for us.

Special thanks to Hugh Johnson of First Albany Corporation for his suggestions on the manuscript.

Thanks also to Michael Cohn, who helped me out tremendously and left no doubt why people consider him one of the classiest, top literary agents around.

Contents

The Whiz Kid of
Wall Street's
Investment Guide

CHAPTER ONE

Three Principles of Stock Market Wisdom:
So Simple a Kid Thought Them Up

Awakened by a Crash

My fascination with the stock market was born on a day many people thought Wall Street had died: October 19, 1987.

I've always kept up-to-date on current events such as the dangers of nuclear war, the troubles in the Middle East, the greenhouse effect. But nothing ever amazed me as much as the stock market crash. It astounded me that in a single day the Dow Jones Industrial Average could plunge 508 points. Not only that, it was impossible to understand how $560 billion could just vanish into thin air.

The media dubbed that day Black Monday. I refer to it as My Great Awakening. It was the day I decided to learn everything about stock investing.

I was nine years old.

The stock market obsessed me. If my mom and dad were looking for me, they knew to check our local Charles Schwab office. I loved hanging out there, watching the ticker run across the wall. I figured out how to pull up loads of market data from Schwab's public Quotrons. I also went to the library a lot to get books on investing and to find information on public companies.

I had gigantic dreams. My goal was to follow in the footsteps of billionaire investor Warren Buffett or legendary stock picker Peter Lynch. I was itching to get started.

But my dad wasn't crazy about my big ideas. In his Confucian style, he told me to be patient. He forced me to educate myself further about the stock market. It wasn't until I was fourteen that I was finally allowed to make an actual investment. I put $700 from my grandparents into a great stock, Cybertek, a business in Dallas that makes software for insurance companies. Since I was too young to invest legally my dad placed the order for me. It was a good pick. Over the next three months, we watched Cybertek climb 114%.

My choice of Cybertek won me some respect from my dad. But I still had to convince him it wasn't just dumb luck. I impressed upon him that I'd put hard work into picking that company. I showed him how I analyzed the company fully after reading an upbeat article about it in a computer magazine. I evaluated the price-to-earnings ratio and the book value, assessed the growth rate, and put it all together with an appraisal of the general tone of the market. I wanted him to know how my mind worked. Eventually he saw the light and agreed I had the knack for investing. Other winning stock picks followed Cybertek as I sharpened my investment techniques. Later in this book, I'll detail for you how I found my other stocks. I hope my case studies will help lead you to your own successful picks.

Beating the Pros

When I was fifteen my dad allowed me to put together a private mutual fund for my family. I wrote a detailed prospectus outlining the fund's investment strategy, its risks, cost per share and anticipated returns. I put my reputation on the line: I named this new investment opportunity the Matt Seto Fund.

It was no picnic wheedling money out of my sisters, uncles, and cousins. They all knew about my success with Cybertek, but they still held on to their money. At last they gave in, not because they wanted to invest but because I was so pushy. I wanted their money, and I wanted it bad. If they said, "Maybe," or "I'll get back to you," I always followed up with a phone call to remind them I wasn't going away.

My cousin Harry wrote me a check for $500. But he warned me if I lost his money I'd mow his lawn for the rest of my life.

In all, I rustled up about $23,000 to kick off the fund. My dad pitched in with about half. By Wall Street standards, I know that's not a lot of money. But I've always believed that it's not how much money you have but how you invest it. Not everyone has millions to throw into stocks—my family certainly doesn't. But whatever amount you scrape together, you want the best return. The real test of any investment strategy is its percentage gain.

I am glad to report that my cousin Harry still pushes his own lawnmower. I haven't lost a penny of his investment. In fact, he's richer thanks to me.

From its start, my fund has consistently returned more than 30% a year. In 1993, when I was fifteen, the Matt Seto fund gained 38%, outperforming 90% of all mutual funds in the aggressive growth category. In 1994, at age sixteen, I managed a return of 33%, beating 99% of the mutual funds in my category. My fund has an annualized average return of 34% through the first quarter of 1995.

I'm especially proud of my performance in 1994. You probably remember that as a dismal year for the stock market. Most people struggled to break even. Many stocks suffered sharp declines. For the year, the Dow industrials gained just 2% and the average mutual fund showed a loss.

In March 1994, *The Wall Street Journal* heard about what I was doing and sent a reporter to find out how a teenager could produce such strong returns. In a front page article, the newspaper said that my performance put the Wall Street pros to shame. After the article ran, I got a ton of mail and phone calls. Investors from all over the world offered me money. All told, I got pledges of about $1 million for the Matt Seto Fund.

My eyes were bulging. But my dad brought me back to earth. He reasoned that managing a million dollars of other people's money was too great a responsibility for a sixteen-year-old kid. He didn't allow me to accept a single penny. Again he said, "Study more, be patient."

The article had other repercussions. Not everyone liked to be outperformed by a sixteen-year-old kid. I got some flak from the regulars at the Schwab office in Troy where I hung out. The regulars showed up there to pass the time, tell jokes, and talk about their wins and losses. When one grumpy grandpa asked me how my fund was doing, I just told him my latest calculation. At that time I was up about 40% on the year.

"Rather surprising," he said with a smirk.

I wasn't surprised at all, but I didn't argue with him. I knew his type. He was from the old school and thought that the only people smart enough to pick good stocks were adults in fancy ties and $200 shoes. He thought that a kid didn't belong anywhere near a Quotron.

When I started investing I expected to do even better than a 30% annual return. I have always thought big. When I first learned about money I wanted to be the richest man on earth. After I learned a little bit about economics I wanted to be a Nobel Laureate. So when I began investing in the stock market I honestly expected returns of 50% or more. To my dismay, I quickly learned that to achieve a 50% gain you either had to invest flawlessly or take huge risks.

Even though I have always set the biggest goals I can imagine, I'm not obsessive about attaining them. Sometimes I can reach them. Sometimes I can't. I know that sometimes settling for a little less is all right. I realize it's pretty good to notch up gains in the neighborhood of 20% to 40%. You can hit that even with a few mistakes.

I had another reason for lowering my expectations. I was investing other people's money. And it wasn't just anybody's money—it was my family's. I definitely didn't want to mow my cousin's lawn forever. Not only that, I didn't want to give heart attacks to everyone in my family. So I scaled back my lofty ambitions. I figured out ways to get substantial gains but keep the risks low.

Developing a Sound Approach

Stocks are simpler than most people think.

What I propose to do here is tell you how I approach investing. You'll see, I think, that my approach to stocks has a lot in common with my approach to life. I'm only a teenager, but I've learned a lot about the stock market and I've just put it all together with some common sense. My method is pretty simple.

In the first place, forget the widespread notion that the top stock pickers are innately the smartest people you'll ever meet. That's pure propaganda. Good investing rests less on raw intelligence than on developing a sound approach.

I venture to say that just about anybody can be a successful investor by following my three simple principles:

1) *Educate yourself.*
2) *Think independently.*
3) *Be logical.*

If you hope to earn any money in the market, you have to educate yourself. You must learn everything you can—not only about investing but also about current affairs, history, and economics. That's not all. You have to know what's going on at the shops in your local mall. What stores are people talking about? Where are customers jamming the doors? Keep your eyes open and absorb as much information as you can.

While you want to be aware of all the latest developments, you need to study them with a discerning, independent eye. You probably hear a lot about jumping on market trends. But if you ride the bandwagon on the way up, you're just as likely to tumble with it on the way down. My firm belief is that it's much wiser to seek your own path. Be original. Discover good solid companies that the crowd may be ignoring in its rush for the latest fad.

It may sound obvious but it needs to be said: In all your deliberations about the market, use your head. There is no substitute for logical thinking. If you keep your wits, and think things through carefully, you're bound to avoid painful mistakes. Careful reflection and common sense will amply reward you.

My investment philosophy is contained in those three principles. My goal is to help you grasp what they really mean. It'll take me the rest of this book to show how I came to rely on them. I'll take you through my learning processes. You'll see how I acquired my approach to investing. I'll open up my mind to you so you can see how I think when I'm picking and trading stocks. I hope the discussion proves illuminating. After all, I began studying the stock market not long ago as a complete novice. As you trace my path from child know-nothing to expert, I hope the road signs I followed will point you in the right direction, too.

Stocks Are like Baseball Cards

The Next Mickey Mantle

Most kids in the fourth grade only look at their local newspaper for the comics. But after Black Monday I pored over our paper for the stock tables and all the other market reports.

My dad had already told me everything he knew about the stock market, which wasn't much. Long before the crash, I remember asking him what a stock was, and he explained it as best he could. He compared stocks to baseball cards. Neither he nor I knew it at the time, but it was really a good analogy.

Kids understand how the value of baseball cards changes but they don't have a clue about what happens in the stock market. Yet the two are similar in many ways. In the first place, you can collect baseball cards and buy stocks for the same reasons: to make money *and* have fun. Of course, everybody wants the cards of the best baseball players. Likewise, you want to invest in the best companies. The value of the cards rises as the players perform well, just as the value of the stocks climbs as the companies prosper. Both in baseball card collecting and in stock investing, you hope to acquire the best long-term prospects. You want to hold on to your cards and stocks for the long haul, hoping in both cases you found another Mickey Mantle.

That was how my dad explained the stock market to me. It wasn't totally sophisticated but it made the point surprisingly well, considering my dad was never very interested in financial matters. To him, money was needed only to pay the bills and properly look after the family. It wasn't important otherwise.

So Confucius said.

But I needed more information than I could get from either my dad or our local newspaper. By the fifth grade, when I was ten, I'd moved on to *The Wall Street Journal, Fortune, Forbes*, and *Barron's*.

I read the financial press because it was fun. I've always been unlike my dad in one big way. I want money. I don't deny it. But I also know I'd never be involved in the stock market if it wasn't just so much fun.

Buying and selling stocks is like playing a good game of Monopoly. The only difference is, winning in the market isn't just a roll of the dice. It's what you know that counts.

PRINCIPLE 1:

Educate Yourself

My parents have taught me to value education. Our family clings to many aspects of traditional Chinese culture, such as Confucian thought. One of the tenets of Confucianism is that education is a vital, lifelong pursuit. It is a noble undertaking aimed at nourishing your mind and improving your character. It should have nothing to do with the grubby world of moneymaking.

In a sense I neglect Confucian values by using my education for the pursuit of wealth. Confucius wouldn't like that. Sometimes my parents don't, either.

Nonetheless, I do have an unquenchable thirst to know what's going on in the world. I'm not interested in being informed only about business and finance. An investor can't afford to miss any news, whether it's from Washington, London, Tokyo, or Katmandu. It could have an impact on your decision to invest or not and, more important, on your success.

Besides newspapers and magazines, I read a lot of books on investing. I'll tell you briefly about them now. You'll hear more about them later when I discuss specific aspects of smart investing.

Four books have had the biggest impact on me.

- *One Up on Wall Street,* **by Peter Lynch**
- *The Intelligent Investor,* **by Benjamin Graham**
- *Capital Ideas: The Improbable Origins of Modern Wall Street,* by **Peter L. Bernstein**
- *The Money Masters: Nine Great Investors, Their Winning Strategies and How You Can Apply Them,* by **John Train**

Peter Lynch has had the biggest impact on me, since his book was one of the first investing guides I read at a very young age. He gives simple, commonsense advice on how to evaluate a company. By now, everybody should know his obvious but brilliant rule: "If you like the product, you'll love the stock."

Benjamin Graham also had a huge influence on me, though I don't rely on many of the same measures he did to gauge a stock's outlook. He relied strictly on a company's numbers to determine whether or not to buy the stock. I think it's important to analyze both the numbers and various intangibles about a company. You have to add a subjective view of the company to the numbers analysis to come up with a thorough picture of the stock. But don't get me wrong: There is no minimizing the importance of Graham's books, *The Intelligent Investor* and *Security Analysis*. He is considered one of the greatest market players of all time and the father of value investing, an approach in which you buy stocks whose prices undervalue the companies' assets.

Though Peter Bernstein's book had less of a direct influence on me, it has helped me figure out how to research stocks and how to think about the market in general. I consider it an excellent history of the investment theories that have shaped Wall Street. John Train's *The Money Masters* examines the styles of twelve great investors including Warren Buffett, Benjamin Graham, Philip Fisher, John Templeton, and T. Rowe Price. Train broadened his analysis of great investors with another book, *The New Money Masters*, which offers insight into the brilliance of people like George Soros, John Neff, James Rogers, Peter Lynch, and Michael Steinhardt. I found the books to be highly educational. They sharpened my knowledge of how to size up companies and weigh risk. By reading these books you learn why the masters follow certain approaches and reject others.

These books, and others, put me on the road to understanding stock market investments. I became aware of the credible strategies and the many gimmicks people use to try to make money on Wall Street. I never relied on trial and error to test each method. I prefer to use common sense to pick and choose from everything I learn.

I don't have a comprehensive theory that allows you just to plug in the variables. That would be boring. No one can rely on a blind routine to become a great stock picker. You have to use your head.

Forget Labels

The Wall Street pros who have to define everything would call my style growth-stock investing. We'll discuss this kind of investing extensively later, but in general it means that I normally seek out undervalued growth stocks. Growth stocks are those that have consistently strong earnings regardless of the condition of the economy. Traditionally, drug companies have been regarded as terrific growth stocks because people needed their medicine no matter what was going on in the economy. So the companies' earnings were always improving at a high rate.

Though I prefer growth stocks, I don't like to restrict myself. If I find a cyclical stock that looks cheap and has good potential, I'll buy it. Cyclical stocks are those that are sensitive to changes in the economy. Automakers are a good example, because their earnings rise or fall depending on the health of the economy. When times are tough, people tend to hold off buying cars, so automakers' earnings slump. In better economic times, consumers will buy more cars, helping to boost the automakers' income.

Earnings are key to a company's stock performance. Good earnings attract investors and drive up the price. Everybody wants to own a piece of a company that's raking in the dough. By contrast, weak earnings turn investors off and hobble the stock price. Who's going to invest in a company that turns a piddling profit?

I learned early that good stock market investing requires some understanding of economics. What happens within the economy invariably affects the companies you're likely to invest in. It's good to have an idea about how economic currents shift.

I sought out books on the great economic thinkers and came away astounded by the breadth and impact of their ideas. Economics, of course, doesn't only affect the stock market. It is the foundation on which our society is built. It underpins everything from politics to race relations to the environment.

I am dazzled by the brilliance of the great economists, people like Adam Smith, Karl Marx, John Maynard Keynes, John Galbraith, Milton Friedman, Paul Samuelson. All of them excite me because they truly are or were what I strive to be: broadly educated, creative, and logical.

Running Roadblocks

It's one thing to acquire general investment knowledge from books and periodicals. It's quite another to ferret out the specific, up-to-date information you need to make real investment decisions. Good investing requires another type of self-education beyond book learning. You need to know how to dig up nitty-gritty details on companies you will potentially invest in. I'll talk about this much more in my discussion about analyzing companies.

One thing worth pointing out now is that collecting information takes incredible persistence. In my case, I not only had the disadvantage of being young and inexperienced in financial sleuthing. I was also handicapped by all the restraints that my parents imposed on me. For a long time, they tried to steer me away from the stock market. If I wanted to be in business, they said, why not become an accountant? They worried I'd end up a broken man and penniless if I became a stock trader. To them Wall Street was nothing but a giant casino.

To curb my ambitions, my dad laid down tough rules. He gave me no money to buy financial books and periodicals. It all had to come out of my own pocket. He didn't allow cable TV, so I couldn't watch CNBC's financial programs. I was prohibited from using my computer to get financial data or business news.

The restrictions taught me to value information all the more. And I came up with some creative ways around them. First, there were Schwab's public computers. It was inevitable I'd become a regular there.

Since I didn't have nearly enough money for all the publications I wanted, I often found myself at the library. I soon realized the library contains everything that the modern investor needs. The selection of newspapers and magazines is fabulous. Not only that, investors can dig up companies' financial numbers in the library's collection of Value Line and Standard & Poor's reports. You can also get tons of annual reports and companies' 10-K filings with the Securities and Exchange Commission. The library is loaded with invaluable information for the stock picker.

I'm grateful my dad took a strict line with me. His rules forced me to make the most of my available resources. I see his strictness as a key lesson in my stock market education. Thanks to his firm hand, I learned my way around the library and honed my research skills. I acquired a lot of knowledge that I might have missed under easier circumstances. I can honestly say that a third of my winning stocks would never have entered my mind if I'd never set foot in the library.

PRINCIPLE 2:

Think Independently

I've had a lot of heroes over the years. For example, when I was eight I admired Ronald Reagan. Every third grader wants to be either president of the United States or a professional baseball player. My first true hero was Donald Trump. From the perspective of a little kid, he had it all: millions of dollars, a glitzy life-style, a yacht, and a permanent spot in high society. I was a sucker for all his novelties. I bought his books and Trump, the game. I still admire him but with less passion. I've realized our paths point in different directions. He's into real estate. I'm into stocks.

Other heroes, besides Peter Lynch and Warren Buffett, are Fab Five basketball player Jalen Rose of the University of Michigan Wolverines and chess champion Bobby Fischer. I like Jalen Rose because he's fearless. He has an aura that separates him from everybody else. He's not only a great basketball player but he's great when it matters: in the clutch. As for Bobby Fischer, I love his determination. People who know him say he thinks about nothing except chess. He plays seventeen chess games a day—he lives, breathes, and eats chess. When a reporter once asked him if there was anything he felt he didn't do enough of, he replied, "Play chess."

What I like about all my heroes is their sense of self-confidence. They never doubt any move they make; they do what it takes to win, and they're brilliant under pressure. Stock market investors could learn a thing or two from them.

Hero worship is fun and exciting. But nobody has had a bigger impact on me than my dad. From him I've absorbed a valuable trait: the ability to think independently, one of my key stock market principles.

A tough life taught my dad to be independent. He was born in south China but at age six fled with his family to Hong Kong shortly after the communist revolution in 1949. When he was seventeen he set off alone to America in search of the American Dream.

He landed in Detroit and worked as a busboy and waiter to pay his way through high school and college, living for a while in a church and then in a tiny room above a restaurant. After working at a few engineering firms, he broke out on his own. Running his own engineering firm, he doesn't answer to anyone except himself. It's a lot of work but it's worth it because he's completely independent.

My mom has known hardship, too. Her father died in World War II when she was three years old. He was one of a long line of Hong Kong sailors in her family. While ferrying war supplies to England, his ship was torpedoed by German submarines. His death left my grandmother financially strapped. Though my mom was a star student, she couldn't attend a fancy university because her family couldn't afford it. So she had a less expensive education and became a nurse. Eventually, she and my grandmother emigrated to Canada. My grandmother lives with us.

My sisters and I are all completely different. My sister Catherine has a surpassing talent for the arts. At age fifteen she was already an award-winning pianist and painter. When she was eighteen, she was one of fifty-two artists to be honored by the National Foundation for the Advancement of the Arts. She took an art degree at the University of Michigan and is now working on her master's in creative writing there. She also has a grant to write a novel.

My other sister, Christine, is the most academically gifted of the three of us. Though all of us are sharp mathematicians, she grasps science with an ease Catherine and I never knew. She's at the University of Michigan studying to be an engineer.

In a family as diverse as ours, you grow up with a healthy sense of your individualism. We always knew what we wanted. We weren't shy about pursuing our interests. As a result, I was exposed to a wide range of ideas. Not only that, I was encouraged to follow my own instincts and, most important for a stock investor, distrust the crowd.

Every Kid a Yo-yo

If my sister Catherine demonstrated her aptitude at a young age for painting and drawing, I showed a natural inclination for business. I set up my first venture when I was ten, and I went a little further than the typical lemonade stand.

At that time, yo-yos were a huge fad at my elementary school. And if you were serious about yo-yos you couldn't have just any brand. It had to be a Duncan. So many kids wanted Duncan yo-yos that they were in short supply in our area. So I searched around a little and found a store a few miles away that had an inventory of the hot item.

I immediately put my operation into high gear. It worked like this: Whoever wanted a Duncan yo-yo placed an order and paid up front, plus a commission and gas money. Once a week I gave the orders to my mom who drove to the store and picked up the yo-yos.

It was pretty successful. No one knew where I got the things. Even if he did, no elementary school kid was going to walk all the way there by himself. He'd have to beg his mom to drive him. So all things considered my prices were actually a bargain.

In all, I made about $20, which was a lot of cash for a ten-year-old. But the lessons I learned were far more valuable than the money. In a broad way I grasped the principle of supply and demand. But I also gained insights explicitly useful in stock market investing.

My Duncan yo-yo enterprise taught me to be creative and original, to keep an eye open for unexplored opportunities. By that I mean: If you see the potential in something, go for it. But do your research. Discovering what no one else knew—that Duncan yo-yos were plentiful nearby—clinched the success of my kiddy effort.

Looking for Excitement

I hang out with friends who always try to be original. Some people might label them as alternative. They're either members of garage rock bands or really into skateboarding. On Friday and Saturday nights we try to entertain ourselves. Let's face it, suburbia doesn't offer a lot of excitement for teenagers. Troy is a pretty stereotypical suburb about thirty miles north of Detroit. It's a lot of housing developments with tract homes. So my friends and I often walk around neighboring Royal Oak, which has an actual downtown with record stores, clubs, and coffeehouses.

I identify with my group of friends partly because we grew up together but mainly because we all try to be as creative as possible. We take an imaginative approach to life. My friends apply imagination to their music and I use it in stock picking. For a long time they had no idea I was involved in the stock market. It was my secret passion. A teenager's life and stock investing didn't normally go together in the eyes of most people. So I kept them separate.

Though I'm ambitious and have already had great success in the stock market, I'm still a typical midwestern kid. My parents' roots may lie in China, but I was born and raised in Troy, Michigan. I feel lucky to be a product of both my family's Confucian philosophy and midwestern values. The ethical demands of Confucius perfectly complement the plain and sturdy views of the midwesterner. Though I may ridicule Troy, I love it for its ordinariness much the way Warren Buffett loves Omaha.

PRINCIPLE 3:

Be Logical

Maybe the most elusive part of my approach to investing is the requirement to be logical. Philosophers have written complicated treatises on the nature of logic. I don't mean to imply philosophical logic at all. And you don't need to know fancy mathematics, calculus, or quantum physics. The incomparable Benjamin Graham said that if you're using anything more complicated than algebra to evaluate stocks then you're doing something wrong. And I think even algebra is largely unnecessary.

What I mean by logic mostly boils down to common sense. The top stock pickers use orderly thought processes. How they make their decisions can be clearly traced from point A to point Z.

Being logical also means taking the time to let your mind travel the full distance from A to Z. Hasty decisions are not logical ones. Many people simply accept the word of their brokers without analyzing the advice. That's not sensible. It astounds me that some people spend more time thinking about what kind of pizza to order than they do about investing $10,000 in a touted stock.

You must employ your logic to understand a company and its prospects. Sometimes this simply means grasping what a company does and how consumers view the product. If you're a camper perhaps you can identify the best boot for the money. In doing so, you may have made it to step A in the search for a good stock.

Now marshal your logic to carry your analysis to the next step. If it's the best boot for the money, then perhaps you've identified one of the strongest boot manufacturers. Do you notice a general trend that points to growing boot sales? If so, and if you really think this is the best boot around, then you may be pointing toward a conclusion. Do you see ads for this boot? Are people talking about it?

It's possible you have identified a coming sales burst for this boot months before the Wall Street analysts start singing its praises. If you're right and you buy now, you may be handsomely rewarded. And then you can pat yourself on the back for using simple logic.

I've always been fascinated by the decision-making process. Of course, the best decisions result from the careful use of logic. But just consider how many decisions we make in a single day and how we use our logic in so many different ways. I've often wondered what lies at the root of all our decisions. Why do we make the decisions we make?

The answer is incredibly simple. Every decision we make is meant to maximize our own happiness. It might be as ordinary as the decision to have dinner delivered from the local pizza joint. Or perhaps it's the decision to buy your girlfriend the nicer necklace. You thought it through and arrived at the logical conclusion that the few extra bucks made sense because it makes you happy to see her happy.

Buying stocks is a part of the daily decision-making process we all experience. It should not be seen as a gigantic hurdle. Remember the same rules apply in deciding whether or not to take an umbrella to work: Think things through carefully, weigh the options, assess likely outcomes, and reach a considered conclusion. Your happiness depends on your decision—no matter if you're buying 300 shares of Ford Motor Company or trying to stay out of the rain.

Sometimes, though, logic is deceptive. Something that is logical may not appear that way at all. For instance, how could I have first become enthralled by the stock market just at the time when it looked as though it was crumbling? If the aim of investing is to make money, why did I see the enormous prospects when everyone was losing money faster than ever?

Maybe it was perverse logic. But I sensed quickly that the 1987 crash presented a wonderful buying opportunity. Stocks were cheap. Unless you had no faith in America and its economic system, there was no reason to stay away from the market. And I was right. I watched stocks climb for the rest of the year. Remember I was only nine years old and didn't have a penny invested, but I knew where I wanted to put my money if I ever got any.

Winning on Wall Street didn't look that tough.

CHAPTER THREE

What the Long Term Looks like to a Kid

Patience Is a Virtue

Certain stereotypes about kids are true. We are impatient. We have short attention spans. We change our minds all the time. We don't like waiting around for things to happen.

In my early days, short-term investing seemed the only way to go. I just couldn't see sticking money anywhere for thirty years, or even two years, for that matter. To a kid, two years is an eternity.

How could I be expected to lock up my meager funds when my only recourse if I fell short was to beg for a few bucks from my parents? Besides, I had so little money that to turn it into anything substantial would take an eternity. And anyway, why would any kid want to invest when he could spend the money on a tennis racket or stereo and actually use the things right now?

It also seemed to me that short-term investing was the way to riches. Don't forget Gordon Gekko in *Wall Street*. He made millions in a matter of hours. Everywhere you turn you see a book or magazine screaming: "How I Turned $500 into $3 Million in Just Three Weeks!" These were mighty temptations for a kid with big ideas.

You probably think a kid like me would be a reckless investor. Think again.

There's another side to kids. Because of our youth, we have the luxury of not being in a race against time. That's the philosophical reason a kid like me can appreciate a long-term investment strategy.

Warren Buffet and Peter Lynch cured me of my misconception that you had to turn over your stocks with fabulous returns in short periods of time. Warren Buffett has made his fortune in long-term investments. He's now considered one of the greatest investors in America—not to mention one of the richest. Best of all, he doesn't come from money, either. I learned a lot from him, and the proof of his style was in my profits. When I was an idiot trader I would buy 100 shares of a stock like Electronic Arts at $21. Then I'd sell it at $23. Then I'd wait for it to drop to $21.50 and buy it back again.

It may look like I knew what I was doing and was making money. But in fact my profits were minimal, especially after factoring in brokerage commission costs.

The superiority of buying and holding came home to me when I watched the video game maker Electronic Arts climb from $21 to $30. If I had just held on after first purchasing the stock at $21, my profits would have been higher.

After that, I quit short-term trading. The benefits of the switch to a long-term strategy were soon reflected in my monthly brokerage statements: my profits increased dramatically. Never forget: Time is your friend in the stock market.

I wish I'd been around in 1919 when Coca-Cola went public. If I'd bought just one share at $40 and then reinvested all dividends and kept all the additional shares I gained from stock splits over the years, I'd be a rich man. By August 1995, my $40 investment in a single share would have grown into 47,904 shares worth $3.2 million. A gain like that proves one of my dad's aphorisms: Patience is a virtue.

Not everyone has the foresight to buy a company like Coca-Cola and hold it forever. But everyone does have the opportunity to benefit in some way from long-term investing. If you're middle-aged or in your golden years, your best bet is to buy and hold. Even a five-year time frame is far better than the minute-by-minute outlook popular among many investors these days.

Consider this: If you had owned all the stocks in the Standard & Poor's 500-stock index in every year since 1926, you'd have gotten an average return of 10% a year. That's even with some horrible years such as 1931, when the index lost 43%.

Buying for the long term frees you from watching the market's daily traumas. Every night the newspapers and the TV news report the latest fluctuation in the widely followed Dow Jones Industrial Average. Sometimes the market barometer swings with such violence that you wind up feeling personally battered yourself. But if you have invested for the long term in solid companies, the daily dance of the Dow industrials is a mere sideshow.

Why get yourself into a panic over short-term price movements when most people agree they're just random? If Shakespeare had been a Wall Street analyst instead of an Elizabethan bard, he might have described these daily flip-flops as sound and fury signifying nothing.

Leave the hair-pulling to the big-money Wall Street traders. They pounce on every market quiver in search of quick profits. Of course, they risk quick losses, too.

Brief market gyrations merely reflect the psychology of the investor crowd. By contrast, long-term price movements are the direct result of a company's performance. If you choose strong companies, they will grow over the years and their stock prices will climb. They will be able to weather tough economic times and bounce back along with their stock prices.

Through Thick and Thin

When you buy stock you purchase a piece of a company. Your financial fate is tied up with the company's destiny. Let's think about this in concrete terms. Suppose your local travel agent sold shares and you bought in. You always liked the travel agent and decided to take the plunge for several reasons: the company's prime location on Main Street with lots of pedestrian and auto traffic; its top-notch selection of tour packages and other services; its terrific management.

But in the first months after you invest, business is erratic. The healthy flow of customers witnessed over the past few years tapers off. It seems many people are worried about a potential economic slowdown and are postponing their vacations. Even business travelers are cutting back on the travel agent's services. Profits fail to increase at the pace of the previous year.

If your time frame were short-term, you'd be worried. But you're looking far down the road. You're convinced of the company's fundamental strength. You decide you're not going to pay any more attention to current conditions. You take your stock certificate and stuff it into the back of your toy box. You leave it there for five years.

By that time, the economy has gone through a couple of cycles. The travel agent has not only survived the downturns but has also expanded in the robust periods. It now occupies three times its original space. Your long-term bet has proved quite profitable. You sell a few shares and telephone the travel agent. You're spending the proceeds on a couple of weeks in Tahiti.

There's another reason to buy and hold stocks. Long-term investors usually hand over less money to brokers in commissions. I learned that lesson the hard way. If you trade often, you need to get higher returns than long-term investors in order to make the same profits. That's because brokers' fees take a chunk out of your returns.

Consider these two scenarios. Long-term Larry, a smart investor, buys $10,000 of Sure-Bet stock and pays a 4% commission to his broker for the privilege of purchasing the shares. He holds Sure-Bet for two years, watching it gain 15% each year. Then he sells the stock and pays another 4% commission on the sale. His total gain, after factoring in what he paid in commissions, is $12,188.16. Now let's see what happens to the investor with a shorter time frame. Short-term Sherman also has $10,000 to invest but he figures the real money is made in a lot of smart trades. Instead of Long-term Larry's one trade, Short-term Sherman makes eight trades over the same two-year period, paying the same 4% commission fees on each purchase and sale. Short-term Sherman had better be a very good trader because in order to match Long-term Larry's gains he needs a 53% return each year after factoring in all his commission fees.

What Are the Chances?

Of course there are always naysayers for any viewpoint. Some studies argue that buy and hold strategies aren't always the wisest. Perpetuators of this perspective like to point out that you could buy and hold for a long period and still perform poorly. These people's favorite example is the fourteen years between 1968 and 1982. If you had owned the stocks in the Standard & Poor's 500-stock index during that period, you basically wouldn't have made a cent. Everybody knows the 1970s was a miserable time for stock investors, but that underperformance doesn't disprove the principle of buy and hold.

Of course, there is an element of timing even in a long-term strategy. But as long as you don't bail out during the down periods, you'll benefit from the historic trend of stock appreciation.

How reasonable is it to assume you'll start a long-term investment program just as stocks begin a long dull period? And how reasonable is it to assume you'll abandon the market just as it's setting off on a torrid run? That's what you'd have to do to satisfy the naysayers.

Sure, it could happen.

But remember the long-term averages are in your favor.

Not only that, stocks outperform other investments over the long haul. After I'd studied the market for a while in junior high, I started wondering if other investments might offer better returns than stocks. To get my answer, I dug up research material on government bonds and Treasury bills.

Stocks won hands down. Since 1926, government bonds have returned 4.8% a year, Treasury bills 3.7%. Compare those figures to the stock market's annual return of 10%. You have to be blind not to see the superiority of stocks.

The Mystery of Stock Price Movements

Lure of Technical Analysis

Wouldn't it be great if there were a perfect formula for picking stocks?

When I started studying the market, that's what I kept thinking. What kid wouldn't? I know a lot of adults think that way, too. You're sure there has to be some simple way to know how a stock price will move. It's just a matter of figuring it out.

Back then I never considered the importance of a company's earnings or its stock price or debt level. A stock just moved for some mysterious reason. If you could crack the mystery you'd be rich in no time.

I thought I'd stumbled upon the solution when I discovered technical analysis. I read a skimpy book on the subject when I was nine. After that, I thought nothing could stop me. Now I was going to amaze the world with my magical ability to predict stock prices. What I gathered from technical analysis is that stock prices basically follow a pattern. Once you understand the pattern you know what the next move will be.

Boy, was I naive.

I'd collected research on a bunch of companies and noticed that every report had a chart showing the stock's performance in recent history. There had to be a good reason to include the chart. I imagined that if you stared hard enough at the squiggly lines eventually you'd see the pattern.

That was the promise of technical analysis, as far as I knew then.

I'm aware now that the technical approach is far more complicated than my nine-year-old brain understood. It takes into account piles of data. It assesses the supply and demand of a stock to determine where the price is going. It also tries to understand investor psychology. Technical analysts believe the mood of market players will influence the direction of stock prices.

Of course, all these factors generally influence market behavior. But technical analysis isn't for long-term investors. If you plan to buy and hold your investments, there is no better way to analyze a potential stock purchase than to look carefully at the nature of the company itself. In Wall Street lingo that's called fundamental analysis, as opposed to technical analysis. In the rest of this book, I'll outline how I use the fundamental approach to pick stock winners.

I didn't accept fundamental analysis right away. First I had to test the technical method. I had to prove to myself it wasn't a magic solution. It was then I first understood there are no magic solutions in stock picking. If you do well, everybody thinks you're a magician; they immediately forget about all the hard work.

So, using technical analysis, I tracked several stocks for a year. I included Mattel and AT&T in my test group. I charted their movements carefully. I dutifully drew graphs. Every week I expected the illuminating pattern to emerge.

Over the year both Mattel and AT&T rose. But I still was no closer to finding any pattern in their advance. I felt incredibly frustrated that the charts revealed no hint of the stocks' future movements.

It was then I sensed that technical analysis wasn't for me. Shortly after my tenth birthday I concluded it was an ineffective system for forecasting price behavior. As a result I eliminated it as a tool for picking stocks.

Of course, I can admit now that there was something else lurking in the back of my mind. Back then I thought maybe technical analysis was just too complicated for a ten-year-old. Yes, you're probably thinking: That makes perfect sense. How's a ten-year-old going to know whether something as sophisticated as technical analysis works or not? Most ten-year-olds have trouble with long division!

True. But a few years later I discovered that others also disputed the effectiveness of technical analysis.

Consider the conclusions of Harry Roberts, a statistician at the University of Chicago's Graduate School of Business. I came across him in Peter Bernstein's *Capital Ideas*.

With statistical thoroughness, Roberts analyzed stock market patterns. His study, written in 1959, suggested that what technical analysts may see as price patterns are really just random movements. His elaborate work further suggested that any systematic patterns that happened to emerge were largely the result of "imaginative scrutiny" by the technical analysts.

That fits with what others have said. In his book, *Stock Market Logic*, Norman G. Fosback says that many people rely on chart patterns in the belief that they reveal the precise times to buy or sell stocks. But, he cautions, the conclusions of the professional chart followers are far from objective. Rather, he notes, reading the charts is largely a matter of personal interpretation.

I'm convinced that technical analysts see price patterns only because they want so much to see them. It's a scary thought but some people actually buy a stock without knowing a thing about the company. These foolhardy souls will invest their hard-earned money barely knowing the company's name, as long as the chart looks good.

Minimizing Risk

It was a good thing I was disillusioned by technical analysis early in life. Otherwise I might never have taken a clear-headed fundamental approach to stock picking. As I grew up, I learned to accept that there are no perfect formulas for successful investing. But I also discovered that nothing paves the way for success better than a good understanding of your potential investments.

It's the same in any situation. Whether you're playing golf or deciding on a new stereo, if you want the best result you have to get a clear grasp of the environment you're in. You have to open your eyes. Touch the grass. Play with the knobs.

In the stock market you have to completely understand the companies you own, or you risk being blindsided. If you are lazy in your research you could wake up one morning to a nasty surprise. Some tiny bit of information you overlook could cost you big.

So it is with marriage, too. If I ever find the right girl, you can bet I'll know everything I can about her before I tie the knot. I hope I'll understand her as much as any company I own. In marriage, as in long-term investing, you want to know what you're getting into *before* you take the plunge. Afterward it's too late. Of course, that doesn't stop some people from marrying virtual strangers. Talk about risk.

My aim in both the choice of my wife and my stocks is to keep risk to a minimum. I'm lucky that I also learned early in my career not to be tantalized by dangerous temptations. I'm referring to a popular trap for novice investors called penny stocks. If any investment flies in the face of sound judgment, it's these extremely cheap stocks. They're companies still in the development stage or in bankruptcy.

The lure is their low price coupled with the usual dream of their enormous potential. Sucker investors believe that any minute now these companies will either produce the world's greatest invention or bounce back fabulously from insolvency.

For a while I, too, was a believer. I thought penny stocks were going to make me an overnight millionaire. I was sure this was a completely logical supposition. The only problem was, it was faulty logic.

Here's how it works—or rather, doesn't. Suppose one of these stocks was selling at the measly price of 25 cents a share. Then consider what kind of gain you have if the price rises by a mere ⅛ of a point. Stocks selling for $30 or $60 jump an ⅛ of a point just at a sneeze. If your 25-cent stock rose an ⅛ of a point, or 12.5 cents, you would be looking at an instantaneous 50% gain. Not only that, imagine how many 25-cent shares you could buy without spending very much money. The potential profits are mind-boggling.

But hold on.

Here's where it pays to step back and think logically for a minute. If you take the time to think things through you'll save yourself a lot of heartache. First, why in the world would a 25-cent stock be more likely to jump by half than would a $30 or $60 stock? The answer is: It wouldn't.

Always remember to think in percentage terms. No stock is likely to jump 50% in a day, except in extraordinary circumstances. Consider this, too: If a stock does show a tendency to swing wildly, it could just as easily plunge by 50%.

Often pure hope fuels these stocks. The companies usually have no product yet, no earnings, huge debt, and a high failure rate. When hope drives a market, despair can be crippling for everyone involved.

And don't think that because you invested only a few bucks you're not risking much. Suppose you sank $100 into the 25-cent stock and it lost ⅛ of a point, or 50%. You may be out only $50. But any way you look at it, you've lost half your investment.

If you were really foolish, or hopeful, you might have thrown $10,000 into the stock. Now your $50 setback is a $5,000 loss. The potential disasters are mind-boggling.

I never did buy a penny stock. But I seriously considered it. I even ordered a few companies' annual reports and researched news articles about them. But as soon as I looked at the fundamentals, I came to my senses.

One company I looked into was Endevco, a diversified energy development concern. But minimal research eliminated it from any consideration. The company, whose stock was trading at 63 cents, hadn't had a profit in three years.

In general, companies without earnings and with poor balance sheets aren't my kind of companies. I'd venture to say that the risky nature of investments in such companies is partly what gives the stock market a bad name. Hollywood, society at large, and even my parents have an image of Wall Street as a giant casino. Once my high school economics teacher preached that success in the stock market was due only to luck. (I just assumed he had a history of bad investing.)

The stock market has a bad rap partly because of the uneducated way some people invest in it. If you approach stocks like a gambler, the best you can expect is a gambler's return. Stockbrokers also must share the blame. Their job often is to sell stocks, not necessarily to research them fully. If a client loses money the broker claims that nothing is a sure bet in the stock market. The client then thinks that if the stockbroker—who is supposed to be well informed—touts a lousy stock, then the market really must be a gamble.

I don't subscribe to those unflattering portraits of the stock market as a casino. I'd even stick my neck out and say that with thorough research, an investor has a good chance of predicting future price movements.

Stocks aren't lottery tickets or playing cards on the blackjack table. Real gambling is subject to so many inscrutable variables that a player really has no chance to control the outcome. Not so with stocks. Research helps define the variables that control stock prices. If you don't do your research you *are* gambling with your money. But if you do your research diligently you can approach investing like a science.

But before we explore the scientific side of investing, a caveat. Since I've already put my neck on the chopping block, it's fair to let me say that no matter how exhaustively you research a company, stock investing is not perfect. Nothing is. Even the most careful chemistry experiments go wrong.

Just ask my science teacher.

Look for Lovable Stocks but Don't Lose Your Head

Open Your Eyes

Buying stocks is a two-step process. First you have to identify a company for potential investment. Then you have to evaluate it carefully.

It's a lot like buying an expensive dress to be worn to a formal dance. Don't get me wrong. I myself have never bought a formal dress. But I do have a mom and two sisters, and they love nothing more than buying fancy clothes. I've seen what they buy and know what they pay, so I'm well aware of the mistakes they make. The mental approach is the same whether you're looking at stocks or sequined gowns.

My mom and sisters start out with the right approach. They shop around. They visit a number of stores and never buy the first dress that looks good. As I do with stocks, they keep notes on the best possibilities. Then, as I do, they evaluate the prices. Is the dress selling in an affordable range? Is it ultimately worth the price? That second question is often the real stumbling block.

Shopping for dresses or for stocks, you can easily fall prey to your emotions. My sisters want to get the best dress for the price. But what happens if they fall absolutely in love with one particular gown? It's just as dangerous as falling in love with a certain stock.

Your ability to reason gets clouded. You may still get a good dress, or a good stock, but you may not get it at a good price. Something worse can happen. Your irrational attachment may cause you to miss certain defects in the fabric (or in the balance sheet). You could wind up buying a lousy dress, or a dog stock, even at a good price.

Worst of all, you could get a horrible outfit or a crummy stock at a lousy price. Then every time you look at yourself in the mirror or read your portfolio statement, you'll groan. So, it's great to like your stocks, but don't fall blindly in love.

Trust Your Instincts

You can reduce the chances of a stock market mistake by simply trusting your instincts to identify good companies for investment. Everybody has the natural talent. If you shop, if you read newspapers and magazines, if you just keep your eyes open wide, you will see amazing possibilities all around you.

A common misconception: Many people tend to look at a company and its stock separately. That's wrong. Good companies make good stocks. Period. Always keep it in mind.

So, you're probably asking, where do good stock ideas come from? My answer is: you, the typical consumer. The best and most obvious way to pick stocks is simply for you to take note of successful companies in your community. A good stock is one that's familiar to you.

The companies that are easiest for the average investor to observe are those that sell their goods and services to us. These are companies you know, ones that satisfy many of our basic consumer needs. They do well when you and I buy their products. If they are especially good at tapping into our desires, then their earnings rise and you can bet the stock will follow right along.

One of my favorites is a company called Best Buy. It operates a chain of stores selling electronic appliances such as video cameras, microwave ovens, and car stereos. I'm partial to it partly because it has made a lot of money for me. It has helped my portfolio shine.

So how did I discover this gem? I first learned about Best Buy when it opened stores in the Detroit area in the summer of 1993. The outlet closest to my house is probably a twenty-minute drive on the expressway.

Best Buy didn't just move into the area and wait for customers to find it. The company advertised heavily in the newspapers and on TV. That got people into the stores. But once they were there, the place had to convince consumers it was a hot spot.

I'll discuss my investment in Best Buy at length as a case study in Chapter 13, but for now I'll say it wasn't long before the store cast its magic spell. Any kid who hadn't walked the aisles felt left out. I begged my mom to take me there. I had to see what all the excitement was about. I thought, how could it be so exciting? It's just a consumer electronics store.

It didn't take a genius to recognize the company's potential. Every time I visited the store, the cash registers were humming. Consumers were dishing out money in a big way.

What made the store so great was that customers, even kids like me, were allowed to try out the merchandise on the spot. You could play around with the TVs, stereos, computers—you name it. Best of all, the store strongly endorsed the concept of No Pushy Salesmen. You could try out video games or listen to music without a salesman bugging you or forcing you to look at things you weren't interested in. You walked into Best Buy and you immediately felt comfortable.

Not only that, the store worked hard to give you the lowest price. Best Buy would refund the difference if you found the same product at a lower price somewhere else within thirty days of purchase. If you brought them proof of a lower price at another store before you made your purchase, they would beat the competition by 10%. Hence the store's name: Best Buy.

All this explains the company's success. Best Buy isn't just another store; it has actually revolutionized shopping for consumer electronics.

My friends and I would always talk about how cool the store was. I was telling myself the stock of this company must be spectacular. It sure was.

I should point out that there was a time when I started to worry a little about Best Buy. But in the end, my worries were unfounded and the experience of watching Best Buy fight for its life gave me a worthwhile lesson about competition.

When sizing up a company, you should always think carefully about its competition. You want your prospective stock pick simply to be the best company in its industry. Its products must outshine its rivals.

Some of the people can be fooled some of the time about some companies. But in the end it's the company producing the best goods and intelligently marketing them that will win. Smart marketing campaigns and snazzy advertising alone aren't enough. They can make a company seem great in the short term, but consumers won't be hoodwinked for long if the advertised products aren't up to snuff. In the technology industry in particular, the truth about the quality of a company's products will always come out in the competition for market share. No matter how heavily the products are promoted, the marketplace will be the final arbiter of success or failure.

It's particularly nice to find a company that has gone head-to-head with competitors in its industry and emerged the victor. I want a company that is dominant in its industry. But I also would prefer one that has already scratched and clawed its way to the top. I feel more comfortable knowing that the company has already proved itself in the rough and tumble world of industry competition.

Not only that, I'm encouraged about the management of a company that has duked it out with the competition and won. Winning reveals a fighter's toughness in management and raises the chances that such a battle-hardened group will likely be able to fend off future onslaughts.

Some companies are lucky enough to dominate their niche without ever having faced a real challenge. Of course, it's wonderful to find a company with little or no competition. But I'd worry if management is yet to be tested in battling incursions onto the company's turf. Remember, if a company is flying high with no competition, you can be sure that the competition will move in.

And that's exactly when I began to worry about Best Buy. It was sailing. It had no serious competition. Its stock price was climbing. Then, sure enough, as it grew ever larger it was forced to butt heads with a pretender to the throne. The challenge came from Circuit City, which built stores in cities claimed as Best Buy's turf. It even put up a store in Minneapolis, where Best Buy is headquartered.

But Best Buy didn't lie down and die. Far from it. The company battled face-to-face with Circuit City, even opening a store in Atlanta, Circuit City's headquarters. And the war was on. Among other things, it took the form of a price war.

The scary part was that stocks of both companies started to fall.

Analysts downgraded the stocks because of the war. The companies' battle for industry preeminence was cutting into profits.

I felt a little uncertain about it all because, to tell you the truth, I had never visited a Circuit City store until about a year into the pitched battle. I read about their outlets and talked to people who had shopped at them. I just kept my faith in Best Buy.

In the end, my side won. Best Buy emerged the dominant company again and, to my eye, the war had left it unscarred. In fact, the company ended up stronger. Because of the competition, the management worked overtime to improve the stores and sharpen efficiency. The battle really showed the strength of the company.

Afterward, Best Buy's stock not only fully recovered but went on to hit new highs.

Great Video Games, Great Stock

You'd expect a kid to know a thing or two about video games. It's like a plumber knowing all about pipes. If a company came up with a new material for pipes the plumber would know if it was promising or not. Or consider a dancer who knows all about ballet shoes. If dancers everywhere start talking about a hot new shoe, the alert dancer would think it was probably wise to check out the company producing the shoe.

But you don't have to be a specialist like a plumber or a dancer to catch a trend. I acquired my knowledge of video games over time. They were something I was interested in. Everybody has special interests. Everybody is a bit of an expert in something. You may not think of yourself that way. But you can use your personal interests to advantage if you look around.

I used what I knew from my daily life to find another winning stock: Electronic Arts. This company makes video games. I got interested in it when I was fourteen because I happened to own a

Sega Genesis video game system. At the time, Sega Genesis was the big competitor to Nintendo, and Electronic Arts made the games played on Sega Genesis.

I quickly realized that Electronic Arts killed the competition in sports video games. Theirs were by far the most fun because they were the most realistic. You felt as if you were actually playing yourself. The computer animation was *that* good. You were there as the Detroit Lions' Barry Sanders broke through a swarming defense, or as the Washington Bullets' Chris Webber slam-dunked on the Phoenix Suns' Charles Barkley, or as the Pittsburgh Penguins' Mario Lemieux streaked off on a fast break in the Stanley Cup Finals.

It was cool the way the company used real players in all its games. Not only that, the games were easy to play. You didn't have to interrupt the fun every ten seconds to check the instruction manual.

One really big hit was John Madden Football. Kids my age had John Madden Football parties that included video game tournaments. Even though we loved the current John Madden game we couldn't wait to see the updated version. We'd call the store and buy it the first day out.

That was a signal the company deserved a serious look. Even a fourteen-year-old kid didn't have to struggle to understand the importance of such enthusiasm for a product.

But Electronic Arts wasn't sailing on just one product. Its other sports video games were terrific, too. The company came up with hits like NHL Hockey and PGA Golf. It was the little things that counted. In football, you could use a variety of real-life plays like a 4–3 blitz on defense or a four receiver run-and-shoot offense. The offensive linemen blocked just like real offensive linemen. You played along as the quarterback saw his receivers downfield, rather than watching from an overhead view as in other games. In hockey you could level a player with a hard check or knock him out in a fight.

Everything, and I mean everything, was as real as it gets. You were part of the action. You were both the coach and the players all at the same time.

The company went beyond sports. There were good action-adventure videos such as the motorcycle game Road Rash, and Desert Strike, where you pilot an attack helicopter in the Middle East. Electronic Arts also makes the hit, Where in the World Is Carmen Sandiego?, a kid's geography game that's seen on public television.

For a long time, every single video game I owned was made by Electronic Arts. It was for a good reason. Whenever I shopped for new games, theirs was the brand I reached for most. From a stock perspective, I had to think that if I liked them so much, there was a good chance others did, too.

Translation: Here was a company that clearly knew how to please consumers. Its reward was likely to be strong earnings and a lofty stock price.

Bingo! Right again.

Electronic Arts had a pretty heady run, from $2.67 a share in 1989 to $42 in 1993, adjusted for stock splits.

Taste of Success

An open mind helped me discover another winning stock. By now, most people have heard of, if not tasted, Snapple iced tea and naturally flavored juice cocktails. This company turned the stodgy iced tea industry on its ear by creating excellent drinks and a wacky advertising campaign.

The Rewards of a Good Stock Pick

Strong climb turns Electronic Arts into one of my best investments

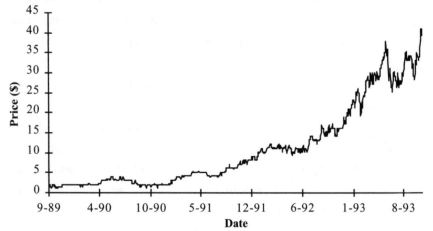

Iced tea was always a middle-aged person's or old fogey's drink. Then Snapple burst on the scene. Suddenly it was okay to be seen holding a bottle of the new hip drink. Snapple brought the beverage to a whole new age group. Long before I tried it, I knew Snapple was attracting a younger crowd.

To me, that was the first sign that this company could be a hot stock. I had a general feeling its products were being accepted by a potent band of consumers.

The second sign was that my own friends were actually guzzling the stuff. Soon I was drinking iced tea flavored with mango or peach. Snapple also enticed us with kiwi-strawberry and "Guava Mania" cocktail juices.

Believe me, I was committed to the big name sodas like A&W Root Beer. I was as anti–iced tea as the next teenager. But I wound up drinking more Snapple than I did anything else. I actually enjoyed it. I got to thinking that if this company could tear *me* away from my favorite sodas, it must be a phenomenon. And, of course, it did prove to be a phenomenal stock.

Beware of One-Product Wonders

An alert consumer knows things that the Wall Street analysts are trying to figure out. The problem with the analysts is that they are more detached from what's really going on in the country than the regular consumers. Or they catch on later than you and I, who just keep our eyes open as we live our lives.

You are the one who knows if you and your neighbors are still shopping at Sears or have switched to Wal-Mart. You may doubt your ability to recognize a great new product when you see it, but at least you can size up whether a store is busy or not.

Yet it's the analysts who really get stocks rolling. If they eventually wake up to what you, the consumer, already know—for instance, that Best Buy's cash registers are humming—they can recommend the stock to all their brokerage salespeople and praise it in reports read by giant mutual fund managers.

Then what happens? All the brokerage clients and money managers wake up to what you already know and pile into the stock, sending it skyrocketing. If you truly were alert and trusted your instincts enough to buy the stock before the analysts started the ball rolling, well, you've not only made a few bucks but you've also proved you're just as savvy as the best on Wall Street, if not more so. It's a great feeling.

Don't be misled, however. Finding great new stocks isn't as easy as it may seem. The road is filled with potholes and wrong turns. For every Electronic Arts or Best Buy, there are plenty of accidents waiting to happen, plenty of companies doomed to fail. These companies usually ride to fame on a popular new fad. They often make one product that happens to be behind the latest craze. Their profits sizzle. The stock soars. But then the fad dies, and any investors who thought they'd found a solid long-term company cringe at the sight of the tumbling stock.

It's important not to confuse these One-Product Wonders with a true gem. Often One-Product Wonders don't have a long-term perspective; their success may lie more with advertising and shifting fads than anything else. Remember Pet Rocks?

A good company, by contrast, will have products with genuine long-term demand. Many good companies were One-Product Wonders at the early stage of their development. The trick is to emerge from that stage. At one point Electronic Arts could have been viewed pretty much as a one-product company. It had a few hit games in its early stages. After that, it could have fizzled. But it didn't. The point is: Some One-Product Wonders can grow into genuinely great stocks, but if you take the plunge and invest early your risk is higher. Your potential reward is, too.

For the investor, I suggest waiting until there are clear signs that a potential stock pick isn't just a One-Product Wonder. If you wait and watch the development of a One-Product Wonder, you can better gauge its real future potential. You may not get in at the very bottom. But so what? It pays to be wise and careful rather than dumb and rash. Even though I got into Electronic Arts after it had already risen a bit, I still turned a tidy profit.

The way to know if you have a true gem or a One-Product Wonder is to subject the company's numbers to real scrutiny, as I explain later in this book. A real moneymaking operation will pass your examination with flying colors. A risky One-Product Wonder will not.

Moreover, a little time and deliberation on your part will allow a company the chance to distinguish itself in another key way: True long-term hits as opposed to One-Product Wonders change the whole direction of an industry. Witness both Snapple and Best Buy. These companies aren't part of mere fads; they don't follow trends. They set them.

Profitable Chats

Alert investors also look beyond the shopping mall for ideas. Do you have friends in a particular industry? Do you trust their judgment of their own companies and others in their industry?

If so, listen to their views. I'm not saying that you should accept their investment advice. Rather, use their knowledge of their jobs and companies to augment your own research. Their views can provide insight into the real workings of a company or industry. Workers naturally know their company's office culture, the expertise of management, the competition. You can apply their thoughts to your investment plans as long as their information is general knowledge. That is, you don't want insider information. Winning in the stock market that way is unfair, not to mention illegal.

As I learned with my yo-yo venture, it pays to use any legal advantage to the fullest. My cousin Harry Yee, the one who threatened me with eternal lawn mowing if I lost his money, used to work at EDS, a subsidiary of General Motors. EDS designs and integrates large data processing and communications systems. While there, my cousin kept his eyes open. He saw how EDS began to attract business from sources other than GM, creating a more stable stream of earnings. He was able to accurately foresee a strong future for EDS.

He made a bundle on the stock.

The chief auto analyst for the Matt Seto Fund is John Vincler. "Auto analyst" may be a bit of a misnomer since I don't pay him. And I have yet to buy an auto stock or a stock related to the auto industry. John, in fact, is a good friend, my former tennis doubles partner. He's sixteen.

We spend a lot of time talking about the auto industry. Astoundingly, he has predicted the last two cycles for the auto business. He's batting a thousand, which is more than I can say for most Wall Street auto analysts who are paid big bucks to know what's going on in the industry.

Remember, he's just a teenager. He has no formal education in business. He hasn't studied the auto industry in any university or in some skyscraper in New York. He just keeps his eyes and ears open.

His chief source of information is his dad, who works at Chrysler. He has long conversations with his dad. And he goes to auto shows and looks around very carefully. He makes his predictions based on what he deduces about the auto companies and their products. He relies very little on macroeconomic mumbo jumbo.

No Absolutes

It's important to remember that the process of selecting stocks is not carved in stone. If there were just one way of picking winners, there would be only one stock market guidebook and everyone would already have retired on personal fortunes made from investing. You must be flexible in thinking about companies and analyzing their numbers. If you're too rigid in your approach, you risk missing an innovative detour to reach your ultimate goal: owning great stocks.

I remember reading a June 1995 interview with University of California at Berkeley economist Paul Romer in *Forbes ASAP*, in which he spoke of the many ways you can manufacture a car. So many different parts go into each auto that the assembly process could be done in a mind-boggling number of ways. He pointed out that a few decades ago U.S. automakers came up with what they thought was practically the best and only way to put a car together on the assembly line.

But then the Japanese began experimenting. "Japanese workers were given the freedom, for example, to try putting the rearview mirror on the door before putting the door on the car, and then to try it the other way around, finding out which was more efficient," Romer told the magazine. "Over time, the Japanese gained a big competitive advantage."

As a result, American automakers began experiments on their assembly lines. They realized that, gee, maybe there isn't a fixed way of doing things. The assembly line process would indeed benefit from flexibility.

Romer's point about auto manufacturing is just as valid for the process of picking stocks: "When you're searching for the best set of choices in a number of possibilities ... you know you'll never really find the best one. There will always be slightly better ones to be found."

In stock picking, there are so many different pieces to the puzzle that there's always a clever and efficient way of adapting the process to your own special style. In the end, the automakers want a solidly built car to come off the assembly line. Just as you want to end up with a sound stock in your portfolio.

There are a million and one ways to reach that end: You need to experiment and to remember that your own unique input into my recommended process is essential.

Cruising the Library

Headline News

My schoolteachers and I don't always see eye to eye. They get annoyed sometimes because I ask so many questions. But I do admit that my sixth-grade English teacher, Mr. Battestilli, made me a better stock picker. Not that he meant to, though. It's just that he made every kid in the class get acquainted with a computer service in our public library called InfoTrac. He thought it would help us do good research. He was right.

InfoTrac gives the headlines of articles published over the last several years on an amazing variety of subjects. Most public libraries now have a computer with the service. It's unbelievable that you can just walk in, sit down and punch a few keys, and find out practically everything that's been published on a subject. And it's free.

InfoTrac is just the first step in researching articles. Since it lists only the headlines, you then have to go find the magazine or newspaper in another part of the library to read the full texts. You're lucky if your library has a big periodical section so that you can find all the articles cited. Some computers have an InfoTrac service that also provides abstracts of the articles.

Some libraries have other services such as Nexis that call up the full text on the screen. That saves rooting around for the actual magazines or going blind staring at microfiche. Your librarian can tell you what resources are available.

At first, I used InfoTrac only for school work. I never thought how great it would be for stocks. If I had to write a report on John Kennedy, for instance, I'd just type in his name and instantly see headlines of every article written about him in the past few years. If there are too many articles to look at, you can break down the information into categories: Kennedy's economic policy, or family, or assassination. For each category, the service lists publications, dates, titles of articles, page numbers, and number of pages. Sure beats leafing through huge catalogs for information.

When it finally hit me to use InfoTrac for stocks I couldn't believe I hadn't thought of it sooner. Once you have a hunch about a possible good stock, I can't urge you enough to head straight for the library computer and check InfoTrac for what's been written about the company.

With InfoTrac and the other resources at the public library you can do just about any research for free. InfoTrac is absolutely ideal for stocks. All you have to do is type in the company name and in a second you see all the headlines about it. You just jot down any articles you want to read about its management, forecasts for its stock, or controversies related to the company. There are usually articles cited that analyze the financial condition of the company and assess its products.

Best of all, you can check out the company's competition. All you have to do is try another search. You type in the competitor's name and then check out the articles about it. That way you can weigh what is said about the competitor against what is said about your stock hunch. Comparing companies is key to making sound investment choices. InfoTrac makes it so easy to do.

But I'd never suggest that you end your research there. Reading published reports about companies is only your first step. And again, you don't even need to leave the public library to take your research further. You can spend several hours wandering around there, and by the end of that time you'll probably have a pretty good feeling about whether or not to invest in a possible stock hunch.

Product Testing

I, of course, was forced to do my research mainly at the library. Because of my father's rules, I had to find a cheap way to get exhaustive information. I can never overemphasize the value of the library. It's perfect for a kid—it costs nothing, has a ton of information, and my parents want me to go there anyway. So everybody is satisfied.

The library has numerous magazines that are indispensable for serious investors. One of the most important is *Consumer Reports*. For those unfamiliar with the publication, *Consumer Reports* is one of the most respected magazines in America. It takes a no-nonsense approach to analyzing and comparing a staggering array of products. It is so serious about maintaining its unbiased reputation that it accepts no advertising.

The staff at *Consumer Reports* tests products extensively to evaluate every facet of their performance. The magazine tells you not only which cars or dishwashers or hair dryers perform the best but also which are the best buys.

You can find *Consumer Reports* at any public library and at almost any newsstand or book store. Reading it will make you a smart consumer *and* smart investor.

What's really great about *Consumer Reports* is that its articles have virtually *no* immediate impact on a company's stock. Unlike Wall Street analysts whose big-mouth pronouncements about certain products or services send stock prices zigzagging, *Consumer Reports* is largely ignored by investors. However, I think the recommendations in *Consumer Reports* are possibly more important than the analysts' views.

That's because a lot of average consumers read the magazine and base their buying decisions on its analyses. They may not buy the products immediately, but they trust the magazine so much that when they eventually do make their purchases they remember the recommendations. As a result, the product evaluations in *Consumer Reports* serve as a kind of long-term forecast for the companies producing the best products.

If you have a hunch about a product and you see it highly rated in *Consumer Reports*, you'd be wise to research the manufacturer very closely. It may be an unknown gem.

For instance, I had a strong hunch about a company called Dura-Craft, which makes humidifiers, heaters, fans, and other home comfort products. I'd done a little research on the company and found that it sells its products at about 250 retailers like Wal-Mart, Sears, CVS, and Macy's. I checked out its balance sheet and saw that the fundamentals were good.

My problem was that I didn't have much day-to-day contact with the products. I don't use humidifiers. I don't buy them. I don't shop for them. So my personal research was limited. Worse, I couldn't find a publication that discussed these products in detail. It wasn't like the computer industry where there's a stack of magazines that analyze every burp in the business.

Following my standard procedure, I scoured InfoTrac for articles about the company. But even that didn't turn up much because DuraCraft is a pretty small company that doesn't get much ink.

I also kept my eye out for the company in *Consumer Reports*, and I got lucky. As it happened, *Consumer Reports* reviewed humidifiers and fans at the time I had DuraCraft on my mind. The magazine ranked DuraCraft's humidifiers and fans as the most effective.

That bit of information tipped the scales. It was what I needed to convince myself that I should purchase shares in DuraCraft. And it is proving a profitable buy. I got in at $33 and watched the stock climb to $41, with the full expectation it would go even higher.

Investment Bibles

Once you come up with a company or two you seriously want to investigate, I recommend checking it out with *Value Line Investment Survey* and *Standard & Poor's Stock Reports*, the bibles of investment services. These resources are best for analyzing bigger companies. Often they don't have much information, if any, on smaller companies. Most libraries carry *Value Line* and *Standard & Poor's*. You can also subscribe to them.

I have found *Value Line* to be one of the best investment services available. Basically, it's a regularly updated publication that contains synopses of companies' operations, their financial numbers, and the service's recommendations.

The individual synopses are extremely useful. They're brief, just a few paragraphs long, but have a broad sweep. You get a sense of a company's business activities and the possible problems and promise that lie ahead.

The numbers section is the best. You can get the same numbers elsewhere but *Value Line* does a little crunching for you that's helpful. I'll go into detail later about what the numbers mean. But for now I'll just point out that *Value Line* contains a figure for a stock's per share book value. By providing that figure, the service has done a little work for you. It's possible to get the number somewhere else, but you'd have to do your own arithmetic. You'd have to find the company's total assets, liabilities, and shares outstanding. Then you'd have to subtract liabilities from the assets and divide that figure by the shares outstanding.

Now wouldn't it be a lot easier to have a peek at *Value Line*? (For example, see page 55 for the *Value Line* analysis of Best Buy.)

Value Line provides a bunch of other numbers, too, including forecasts for revenue and earnings, cash flow, working capital, and so on. The figures are presented in a neat, orderly table that makes it easy to compare year-to-year performances.

Value Line also provides stock recommendations. But as with most stock recommendations, I don't pay much attention to them. Stock recommendations fly at you from all directions—brokers, TV commentators, analysts, newspaper and magazine articles, newsletters, and investment services like *Value Line*. It's a wild and confusing maze of suggestions. I'll describe how to assess recommendations in general in Chapter 9. As for *Value Line*, it recommends stocks using a 1 to 5 scale, with 1 being the best. It zeroes in on two aspects: the stock's risk and the timeliness of buying now.

Another service similar to *Value Line* is *Standard & Poor's Stock Reports*. On the positive side, you can plunge into it for free at most public libraries. On the negative side, I think it's a little more difficult to use than *Value Line* and not quite as comprehensive. Unlike *Value Line, S&P* doesn't offer forecasts or recommendations. The data is mostly historical.

But the *S&P* reports do touch on areas not included in *Value Line*. For instance, you can find some particularly useful numbers

BEST BUY NYSE-BBY

RECENT PRICE	**26**	
P/E RATIO	**18.6**	(Trailing: 21.5 / Median: NMF)
RELATIVE P/E RATIO	**1.31**	
DIV'D YLD	**Nil**	
VALUE LINE	**1682**	

High:	3.2	7.3	7.8	5.1	3.8	4.2	11.8	13.3	31.4	45.3	
Low:	1.3	3.0	1.9	2.2	1.9	1.5	1.8	4.7	10.8	19.0	

TIMELINESS 3 Average (Relative Price Perform-ance Next 12 Mos.)

SAFETY 4 Below Average (Scale: 1 Highest to 5 Lowest)

BETA 1.20 (1.00 = Market)

1997-99 PROJECTIONS

	Price	Gain	Ann'l Total Return
High	105	(+305%)	42%
Low	60	(+130%)	23%

Target Price Range 1997 | 1998 | 1999

Insider Decisions

	A	M	J	J	A	S	O	N	D
to Buy	0	1	0	0	1	0	0	0	0
Options	0	1	1	0	5	0	0	0	0
to Sell	0	0	1	0	1	0	0	0	0

Institutional Decisions

	1Q'94	2Q'94	3Q'94
to Buy	40	55	51
to Sell	43	32	47
Hld'd(000)	31950	30742	29620

Percent shares traded: 45.0 / 30.0 / 15.0

Options: CBOE

Best Buy Co., Inc. was incorporated in Minnesota in 1966 under the name "Sound of Music, Inc." The current name was adopted in 1983. Best Buy began as a retailer of audio systems. Between 1980 and 1984, the company added video equipment, microwave ovens, and major appliances. In April 1985, Best Buy went public with an initial offering of 650,000 shares. In November 1991, a secondary offering of 2,700,000 shares was completed. The lead underwriter was Goldman Sachs.

CAPITAL STRUCTURE as of 11/26/94
Total Debt $472.7 mill. Due in 5 Yrs $345.0 mill.
LT Debt $227.0 mill. LT Interest $21.5 mill.
Incl. $13.8 mill. capitalized leases.
(Est'd Total interest coverage: 3.0x) (28% of Cap'l)

Leases, Uncapitalized Annual rentals $38.9 mill.
Pension Liability None - No defined benefit plan

Pfd Stock $230 mill. Pfd Div'd $14.95 mill.
4.6 mill. 6½% (annual rate) monthly income, convertible 1:1.11 into com. at $45/sh. (29% of Cap'l)
Common Stock 42,165,840 shs. (43% of Cap'l)

CURRENT POSITION

	1992	1993	11/26/94
Cash Assets	7.1	59.9	20.5
Receivables	38.0	57.1	150.0
Inventory (FIFO)	250.0	637.9	1491.1
Other	9.8	13.9	26.5
Current Assets	304.9	764.6	1688.1
Accts Payable	118.4	294.1	787.7
Debt Due	13.3	20.1	245.7
Other	54.3	87.8	134.7
Current Liab.	186.0	402.0	1168.1

ANNUAL RATES

of change (per sh)	Past 10 Yrs.	Past 5 Yrs.	Est'd '91-'93 to '97-'99
Sales	--	25.0%	30.0%
"Cash Flow"	--	23.5%	29.0%
Earnings	--	28.0%	30.0%
Dividends	--	--	Nil
Book Value	--	20.0%	29.0%

Fiscal Year Begins	QUARTERLY SALES ($ mill.) A				Full Fiscal Year
	May Per	Aug.Per	Nov.Per	Feb.Per	
1991	165.6	193.6	230.6	339.9	929.7
1992	246.5	285.5	474.4	613.6	1620.0
1993	441.9	563.0	808.5	1193.1	3006.5
1994	849.4	933.2	1349.9	1867.5	5000
1995	1200	1300	1900	2600	7000

Fiscal Year Begins	EARNINGS PER SHARE A B				Full Fiscal Year
	May Per	Aug.Per	Nov.Per	Feb.Per	
1991	.02	.07	.08	.16	.33
1992	.04	.08	.15	.30	.57
1993	.05	.18	.26	.52	1.01
1994	.10	.18	.41	.66	1.35
1995	.15	.27	.60	.98	2.00

Cal-endar	QUARTERLY DIVIDENDS PAID				Full Year
	Mar.31	Jun.30	Sep.30	Dec.31	
1991					
1992	NO CASH DIVIDENDS				
1993	BEING PAID				
1994					
1995					

	1984	1985	1986	1987	1988	1989	1990	1991	1992	1993	1994	1995	© VALUE LINE, INC. 97-99	
Sales per sh A	--	6.09	9.67	17.79	20.43	20.65	26.75	27.83	46.98	72.03	117.90	150.00	283.50	
"Cash Flow" per sh	--	.25	.38	.31	.39	.45	.50	.58	1.01	1.54	2.25	3.25	6.35	
Earnings per sh B	--	.22	.33	.11	.11	.23	.18	.33	.57	1.01	1.35	2.00	4.30	
Div'ds Decl'd per sh	--	--	--	--	--	--	--	--	--	--	Nil	Nil	Nil	
Book Value per sh	--	.77	2.25	2.36	2.44	2.66	2.28	4.68	5.29	7.46	8.95	11.30	26.60	
Common Shs Outst'g C	--	18.58	24.78	24.68	24.80	24.83	24.86	33.65	34.49	41.74	42.40	43.00	50.00	
Avg Ann'l P/E Ratio	--	10.5	18.0	35.6	27.1	10.4	15.2	20.8	15.1	18.8	Bold figures are Value Line estimates		19.0	
Relative P/E Ratio	--	.85	1.22	2.38	2.25	.79	1.13	1.33	.92	1.11			1.45	
Avg Ann'l Div'd Yield	--	--	--	--	--	--	--	--	--	--			Nil	
Sales ($mill) A	--	113.1	239.5	439.0	506.7	512.9	664.8	929.7	1620.0	3006.5	5000	7000	14175	
Gross Margin	--	25.7%	25.8%	24.9%	24.3%	24.5%	22.5%	20.6%	18.4%	15.9%	14.0%	13.5%	13.0%	
Number of Stores	--	12	24	40	41	49	--	73	111	151	210	260	420	
Net Profit ($mill)	--	4.1	7.7	2.8	2.8	5.7	4.6	9.6	19.9	41.7	62.0	103	215	
Income Tax Rate	--	50.3%	50.6%	42.4%	40.0%	40.0%	38.6%	37.5%	38.0%	39.0%	39.0%	39.0%	38.5%	
Net Profit Margin	--	3.6%	3.2%	.6%	.6%	1.1%	.7%	1.0%	1.2%	1.4%	1.2%	1.5%	1.5%	
Inventory Turnover	--	4.1	4.1	4.1	3.8	4.0	5.5	6.4	6.9	5.7	5.0	4.8	4.6	
Working Cap'l ($mill)	--	12.7	48.7	72.1	74.1	78.4	64.6	126.8	118.9	362.6	490	525	750	
Long-Term Debt ($mill)	--	1.7	6.0	42.8	34.8	35.1	35.4	14.9	48.1	210.8	230	310	360	
Net Worth ($mill)	--	14.4	55.8	58.2	60.4	66.2	56.7	157.6	182.3	311.4	610	715	1330	
% Earned Total Cap'l	--	26.0%	12.5%	4.7%	5.1%	7.3%	6.8%	6.0%	9.0%	8.8%	8.5%	11.0%	13.5%	
% Earned Net Worth	--	28.3%	13.9%	4.8%	4.7%	8.6%	8.0%	6.1%	10.9%	13.4%	10.0%	14.5%	16.0%	
% Retained to Comm Eq	--	28.3%	13.9%	4.8%	4.7%	8.6%	8.0%	6.1%	10.9%	13.4%	15.5%	18.0%	16.0%	
% All Div'ds to Net Prof	--	--	--	--	--	--	--	--	--	--	6%	15%	Nil	

BUSINESS: Best Buy Company, Inc. sells consumer electronics, major appliances, home office equipment, entertainment software, and photographic equipment through a chain of about 210 retail "superstores" located in 27 states. Most stores are located in the Midwest (roughly 45% of store base is located in IL, TX, MN, and MI). Average sales per store in fiscal 1993: $22.6 million. Consumer electronics accounted for 38% of fiscal 1993 sales; home office equipment, 36%; entertainment software, 12%; appliances, 9%; other, 6%. '93 deprec. rate: 9.6%. Has about 9,600 employees, 900 stockholders. Insiders hold 26% of stock; FMR Corp., 10.3%. Chairman & C.E.O.: Richard M. Schulze. Inc.: MN. Address: 4400 West 78th St., Bloomington, MN 55435. Tel.: 612-896-2300.

Best Buy's sales growth continues to be strong ... In January, the company's top line rose by 67% on a 17% gain in same-stores sales. Moreover, for the 48-week period ending in late January, Best Buy's total sales soared 70%, while comparable-store sales grew at a 21% clip. (Fiscal years end in late February.)

... but gross margins have suffered. Best Buy (and other consumer electronics retailers) used promotions to clear out older-model computers through January, causing margins to decline. With a new line of feature-laden, Pentium chip computers in stock, however, some improvement is likely. This is despite the fact that computers—which carry lower margins than other electronic gear—are comprising a larger percentage of this industry's sales. We expect earnings growth to accelerate in fiscal 1995. Assuming that moderately declining gross margins are more than offset by sharply lower SG&A expenses per sales—the result of a noncommissioned sales force and costs spread over a wider base—Best Buy's 1995 share net should reach $2.00, a 48% gain. The stock price has fallen 40% since our late November report. Management's announcement that fiscal third-quarter earnings would not meet expectations, coupled with the above-mentioned margin erosion, knocked the stock price down from near-record levels. This stock is an average choice for the year ahead.

Best Buy has superior long-term prospects. Given its attractive megastore format and the growing affordability of electronic equipment, Best Buy can likely continue its rapid expansion over the 3- to 5-year haul. If so, the nation's second-largest consumer electronics retailer will double its store count and more than triple its earnings by that time.

The recent price decline has boosted this stock's 3- to 5-year appreciation potential. Assuming that our projections out to 1997-99 are accurate, investors are paying a justifiable premium for Best Buy's sustainable 25%-30% top- and bottom-line growth of the past five years. Those averse to the high volatility of these shares and/or seeking income should consider the recently issued convertible preferred issue, currently yielding 8%.
Robert M. Egan   February 24, 1995

(A) Fiscal year end changed from March 31 of following calendar year to Saturday closest to February 28, effective 2/90.
(B) Primary earnings. Excludes loss from discontinued operations: '88, 9¢. Excludes loss from nonrecurring items: '90, $1.69.
Next earnings report due late March. (C) In millions, adjusted for splits. (D) Fully diluted three to five years hence.

Company's Financial Strength	B
Stock's Price Stability	5
Price Growth Persistence	65
Earnings Predictability	45

Best Buy: clearly a winner. Best Buy's growth in earnings and sales translates into a rising stock price. Notice the strong trend in growth of earnings per share and sales since 1988, and how the stock price has also climbed since 1988. The number of stores has also increased dramatically, too.

such as a company's total cash flow and its return on equity.

The *S&P* reports are broken into two sections: the text and the numbers. The text is fairly basic, covering the company's business activities, important developments, and finances. The numbers also include basic data like balance sheet information for the past year.

The Company Speaks

Another good source of information is a company's annual report. This glossy publication details a company's financial condition in the preceding year. Under the regulations of the Securities and Exchange Commission, companies are required to distribute annual reports to shareholders. The report describes the company's operations and shows its balance sheet and income statement.

Many public libraries keep the annual reports of big companies on file. But you can also telephone the company itself and have a copy mailed to you free. I figure if I can get it cheap and for keeps, why not? It's best to get the annual reports for the last few years, if they are available.

The key advantage of the annual report over other sources of information is what it subtly tells you about the company. Every report contains a letter to the shareholder, usually written by the chairman of the board of directors. These letters are often a lot of propaganda, but the way they're written does give you a feeling about the company and its management.

From the letter, you get an idea of what the chairman thinks he should tell shareholders. That, in turn, can give you a sense of what the chairman thinks are the important issues to shareholders. Not only that, he also subtly conveys what he thinks shareholders expect of him. Reading these letters may be as close as you ever get to directly hearing the views of the board chairman of a company you plan to invest your hard-earned money in. As far as I know, no other publication prints the letters.

A lot of people slam annual reports because of their obvious public relations slant. I grant that they are giant advertisements; still, they should not be overlooked. Besides printing the words of the chairman, the report also gives a good explanation of the company from the management's point of view. It doesn't hurt to know why a company thinks its products are superior or why it thinks its stock is attractive. You must remain skeptical, but at least you have a basis from which to start your evaluation of the company.

Some professionals argue that the annual report is the best place to get accurate financial numbers on a company. Sure, they're accurate—they have to be. But annual reports aren't always the most easily understood pieces of literature for the average investor. I find the presentation of numbers to be superior in *Value Line* and *Standard & Poor's*. Those reports give you the most important numbers in an easy-to-read format.

But numbers are numbers. They'll be the same in all publications. As for accuracy, of course a slipup by an investment service could cause you untold headaches. You could work out all your calculations, decide to invest, go out and make your purchase only to discover that the initial data was incorrect. It could happen. But it's unlikely.

Hello, Mr. CEO . . .

Calling a headquarters for an annual report is sound advice, but don't get your hopes up about getting any other information out of a company. If you think anybody is going to answer your probing questions sincerely, you're fooling yourself. After reading a few investment books that urged readers to call companies for information, I did so. Calling seemed logical enough but I soon gave it up, realizing I could better use the time for real research.

It occurred to me that those investment guides I'd read were written by high profile money managers. They were able to get top officials on the phone because they owned a good chunk of the company's shares. Chief executive officers probably called *them* just to make sure the big investors were happy. Moreover, the money manager was just as likely to give the CEO advice on running the company as he was to get information about the company.

If you can get in contact with a reliable source at a company, by all means do so. Good luck. But I don't think it's absolutely necessary to being a good investor.

Many people think you need to know about the president or the chairman to evaluate a company properly. It's as if you can truly understand a company only if you understand the management. I don't buy that idea. How do you evaluate management anyway? On where the CEO went to college? Or how long he's been in the business? Those criteria are of minor significance, as far as I'm concerned. Since few shareholders ever know the management of a company, any evaluation they make is based purely on circumstantial evidence. You can't know how management really operates unless you work for the company or are in the midst of the operation in some other way.

So how *do* you evaluate management when you don't know the top dogs? You look at their effect: the products they turn out and the numbers in their balance sheets. That brings us right back to my original point: that you need to understand what the company does. By understanding what the company does and how it does it, you have your answer to the quality of the management. Good products and good numbers mean good management. The way to measure the effectiveness of the CEO and his cohorts is to carefully study the company's bottom line, which we'll get to in Chapter 7. Understanding the company itself sure goes a long way, especially when the top brass slam the door in your face.

Of course, I've had my own problems when it comes to being taken seriously by corporate officials. Far from getting through to the CEO, I've never gotten past the investor relations office. I must say, however, if you really must talk to *someone* at the company, the investor relations people aren't too bad. Their job is to talk to investors like you. They won't reveal anything crucial, but they can keep you up to date and answer basic questions. But if you're well informed from other sources, you can probably answer these questions yourself.

Beyond the Library: At Home at Schwab

It's not unusual to see a kid my age hanging around the library. It's probably a nice, wholesome sight, even though I'm not sitting there reading about Huck Finn but rather punching my calculator and dreaming about getting rich. Less typical is to see a kid like me hanging out at Charles Schwab. But I go there for the same reason I go to the library—it's a great place to get free information.

Schwab's motto is: Helping Investors Help Themselves, and I take them at their word. I wander around their office as often as I can, helping myself to their resources. I do have my account with them and so I do have a legitimate right to use their information.

At first, though, I just liked to play around with the resources there. I tried the place out after seeing ads for it on TV. Even though I didn't have an account and was very young, the Schwab staff didn't seem to mind having me around.

Of course, the Schwab people assume that if you use their resources, you either have an account there or will set one up when you decide to invest. Without meaning to sound too promotional, I'd say that for the small investor Schwab is an ideal brokerage because of its low commissions and free information.

I can't speak for all the Schwab branches, but as far as I know, most have three sources of information available free to the public. These are *Value Line*, which I mentioned earlier, *Morningstar*, a mutual fund information service that I'll discuss in detail later, and a Quotron, which is a computer packed with stock information in real time (the actual time when trades are taking place).

Quotrons aren't exclusive to Schwab by any means. They're used throughout Wall Street by brokers and analysts, and some sophisticated investors are hooked up to the system at home. It's great to be able to walk off the street and punch into this highly useful device.

An Eye on the Dow

You can find out from the machine where the Dow Jones Industrial Average is trading up to the latest minute, as well as check the level of Standard & Poor's 500-stock index or practically any of the other dozens of indexes that measure various aspects of the market. Not only that, if you punch in an individual stock symbol you can get a real-time quote, including the high and low for the day and year, trading volume, book value, and price-earnings ratio.

Best of all, the Quotron delivers up-to-the-minute news stories. You can read reports on company earnings, some analyst stock recommendations, economic reports, and other articles just as they hit the wires. Wall Street traders look at the same information and swiftly buy and sell based on the flow of news. You can also get some historical information out of the Quotron. You can search for articles on certain subjects and companies released on the wires over the past few months.

As soon as I learned to use the Quotron I was hooked. It's a key tool for any stock investor. If you don't use one, you'll end up ignorant of many facts that are important to your stock portfolio. Mountains of information are contained in the company news releases that are constantly pouring onto the wires. If you don't keep up with this flow, you'll wind up making stock market decisions based on incomplete information.

Imagine that you miss a news release that has a huge impact on a stock you own. Perhaps the release, or the company, is too small to be adequately covered in *The Wall Street Journal* or elsewhere. Sure, you can find out about the news two months later in the company's quarterly report or in data from *Standard & Poor's*. But imagine how much the delay will hurt if by then the stock already has plunged 30%.

I get another valuable resource through Charles Schwab: *Company Research Reports*, available for a fee by fax or mail through Schwab Investment Reports Service. You can get similar services from full-service brokerages; there's no fee but you pay for them anyway through higher commission costs. That kind of service, however, is usually a little more comprehensive.

Nonetheless, *Schwab's Company Research Reports* is without doubt the most comprehensive investment service I use. Its best feature is that it covers many smaller companies that the other services ignore. You get standard data such as the stock's dividend yield, a graph of price performance over twelve months, and details about the company's income statement. It's all broken down clearly and simply for you.

A real bonus is the earnings forecasts in which you get Wall

Street analysts' profit estimates for companies. You even see the number of revisions that analysts make to their forecasts and the extent of revision. That tells you the trend in analysts' thinking about a company's earnings. You also get a look at the average earnings estimate as well as the high and low forecasts.

Strength in Numbers

"Got Any Stock Tips?"

For a long time no one wanted my views on anything. Who cared if I thought the Tigers would win the American League pennant? Even more ridiculous was to ask *me* for guidance on the stock market.

No one listened to me for the simple reason that I was a kid. Everyone assumes most kids don't know a lot about stocks, and that's probably true. But most adults don't know much, either. Still, no one was going to trust the investment advice of a sixteen-year-old.

All that changed after I appeared on the front page of *The Wall Street Journal*.

How nice to get a little respect!

Now everybody asks me for financial advice. I get questions from my parents' friends, from my own friends' parents, my teachers, the high school janitors, and even complete strangers. Everyone asks the same thing: "Got any stock tips?"

Normally I don't like to give out stock tips. Most people won't understand why I recommend a certain company anyway. They might buy it and then not know when to sell. I'd feel terrible if they eventually lost money on my recommendation. Worse, they could end up frittering away their kids' college money or their own nest egg and then come after me with a meat cleaver.

But sometimes people just won't leave me alone until I do recommend a stock. In those cases, I simply mention one of the stocks in my portfolio that I particularly like. More often, though, I try to avoid saying anything concrete. If I *have* to say something—and if I'm determined not to mention a stock by name—I offer the greatest one-line stock tip in the history of stock tips: Buy low, sell high.

Besides being truly great advice, it's a neat line and shows I do have a sense of humor. But I never know what kind of response I'll get. Sometimes people take it as a joke and laugh. Other times they glare at me, emphasizing that they absolutely wanted a stock tip. Then I point out to them that investors who have bought low and sold high have been pretty successful . . . I say, Why don't you see if you can't do it yourself?

Seriously, to buy low and sell high is the best tip I can give anyone. It's better than any specific stock pick. Sure, it's obvious advice. Not only that, it's a standard investment cliché. But get past your prejudice and you discover that the tip suggests far more than you'd expect from a mere cliché.

To Buy or Not to Buy?

The question underscores the importance of studying the financial numbers of a company you're considering for investment. If you want to buy low and sell high, you had better know what a company's financial picture looks like.

After you've done all your qualitative investigation—assessing the quality of the product and the company in general—you need to evaluate the financial side of the company. It's at this point you turn your attention to the quantitative side of your potential investment, the numbers side, which includes the company's debt, inventory levels, cash flow, book value, and price-earnings ratio among other things. Quite simply, you ask yourself, How do the company's financial numbers stack up? The answer to that question helps you reach the most important conclusion of all: whether or not to buy the stock.

If you want to buy low and sell high, it's crucial to remember that you must fully assess a company's numbers. Look at the numbers too narrowly and you wind up with a narrow—and potentially damaging—perspective on the company. You must watch for the trend in the numbers. Not only that, you could limit your understanding of the company if you consider only certain types of numbers, such as the price-earnings ratio, and fail to consider book value. It would also be foolishly narrow not to measure one company's numbers against another's to see whose numbers look better.

If you truly want to buy low and sell high, you must also consider the relative relationship between numbers. If you read the numbers correctly you can usually determine whether a stock is selling at a low price relative to its historical performance. That may entice you to buy. But you also want to determine if the stock is priced low relative to what its potential is, so you can eventually sell it at a high price. The answer lies in the numbers.

Your strength is in knowing the numbers. Only a keen grasp of the numbers can give you the confidence you need to feel comfortable about investing.

Art Versus Science

I get really excited when it comes time to analyze the numbers of a potential stock pick. You can't argue with numbers. When you evaluate a company in terms of its products and management and store appearance, you're in the realm of art. But when you tally up the financial numbers, you've entered the world of science.

Numbers speak to me. First I figured out batting averages for my favorite baseball players like Walt Terrell, Frank Tanana, and Terry Steinbach or scored averages for basketball stars like La-trell Sprewell, Reggie Miller, and Dennis Rodman. When I started going over company balance sheets I got the same thrill watching how the numbers work. I should point out, however, that the only math class that directly helped me analyze stocks was prealgebra. Remember, Ben Graham said you don't need anything fancier than simple algebra to evaluate a stock. For me, math classes mostly helped sharpen my skills of reasoning and deduction.

To be a great stock picker you don't have to love numbers. You merely have to acknowledge their importance in the evaluation process. It also helps if you can do the few simple calculations that I'll show you. But, number phobics, don't fret. Believe me, it's all very simple.

Burden of Debt

I like to start my numbers review with the debt line of a company's balance sheet. You can find the figures in the annual report, *Value Line, Standard & Poor's*, and reports of most other research services. I don't usually spend a lot of time on this number, simply because you can tell right off whether the debt cancels out a company for further consideration. Who wants a company loaded down with debt? It's a sure sign the company isn't as strong as you'd like for a long-term investment.

It's easy to get a picture of a company's debt level. You simply measure the debt against stockholders' equity, which is how much shareholders own of the company. For example, one of my best stocks, Chipcom, had debt of $1 million in 1993 compared with equity of $148 million. So Chipcom's debt wasn't even 1% of its equity, and that's stupendous.

A debt-to-equity ratio like that screamed at me to go on and investigate Chipcom further. Keep in mind that the average ratio of debt to equity is at least 1 to 4, or 25%. Any company that falls into that area merits further attention. Of course, Chipcom proved attractive for many reasons, but its debt level stood out. And the stock performed brilliantly, climbing from $14 to $75.

It's important to note that debt must be measured in the context of a company's industry. Some industries—such as building materials—simply operate at higher debt levels than other industries such as computer software. Some companies run very profitably with a lot of debt. Consider Best Buy, which has maintained a relatively high debt level but has still grown very successfully.

In general, however, high debt decreases the attractiveness of a company. In the first place, it requires a lot of interest payments that can chip away at future cash flow. Payment on interest is money lost that might have been spent on something productive. Companies burdened with high debt also may be more vulnerable than their leaner competitors to inevitable slowdowns.

For me, checking the debt of a company is really like looking at the speed limit signs on the highway. A good debt position says, "Put the accelerator to the floor and race ahead in your investigation." A lousy debt level flashes a warning sign that says, "You'd better slow down and drive carefully."

Peeking into the Warehouse

Another window on a stock's prospects is a company's inventory level. The annual report contains information about inventories but understanding it isn't always easy. The acronyms used to describe the flow of inventories are especially confusing. But don't let that worry you.

The level of inventories isn't as important as the rate of change. Make sure you find out how fast inventories are growing. Compare the latest year's inventories with the previous year. Check the trend over the last few years. The last thing you want is for a company to be sitting on piles of its product. Simple common sense tells you that if the company has warehouses full of its products something is wrong with sales. Not only that, high inventories could hurt future earnings as the company tries to unload its stuff at bargain prices.

What you'd like to see is a high turnover rate for inventories. The less time a product spends in the warehouse, the better the return on the money the company had to invest to build its inventory. Not only that, if products are heading out the door at a fast clip, then sales are obviously good, and future earnings may be bright.

But beware of a company that tries to convince you everything is all right when sales are growing at a slower rate than inventories. If inventories are accumulating faster than a company can get rid of them, then price cuts are inevitable. And lower prices often translate into lower profits.

As with debt, inventory levels need to be viewed within the context of the companies' industries. High inventory for one company may not be as bad for another. In the computer industry, for instance, once a new wave hits, no company wants to be stuck with piles of an old model. If a faster machine comes out and becomes the standard, which can happen very quickly, few consumers are going to buy the slower computers. High inventory levels are particularly risky for fast-paced computer makers.

On the other hand, makers of home comfort products such as fans or humidifiers needn't worry as much about inventory pileups. Revolutions in these products rarely strike with such lightning speed as in the computer industry. So higher inventories may not be as detrimental. I don't know many people who can't live without the latest, greatest version of a fan.

River of Cash

The term cash flow has a nice ring to it. I like to picture hundred-dollar bills floating down a river or spurting from a fountain. Unfortunately, the concept is much more mundane than that. But it's still very important in analyzing a potential stock pick.

The term cash flow refers to the amount of money a company pulls in from doing business. Companies that accumulate a lot of cash without spending a lot to make it are the most attractive. You especially want to target companies that have not only a high cash flow but also one that increases over the years.

You can use cash flow to measure two important aspects of a company. It gives you a good picture of the company's future performance: A lot of cash signals good growth prospects and a company's ability to enhance shareholder value. Cash flow per share (the figure can be found in *Value Line*) tells you whether or not the stock price is attractive: If the cash level is high relative to the price, you've found a stock that's a nice value.

Let's first look at the impact of cash flow on the operations of a company. Just like strong earnings, a healthy cash flow reflects a robust company. Cash is key to smooth operations: You need a steady cash flow to pay regular dividends, to cover your costs for goods and services, to invest in capital improvements and new technology, and to meet interest payments on any debt. Covering all these expenses with cash is a lot easier and more efficient than having to borrow.

Just consider it from the angle of your own household. You need a good flow of cash to pay for food, clothing, and other basic needs. Because of limited cash flow, a lot of people nowadays go into debt for their basic necessities: They use credit cards for everything from gasoline to groceries. Anyone with a mounting credit card bill knows how debt can constrain household operations. Companies, like households, suffer when cash flow shrinks and debt climbs.

If a company has a strong cash flow, you then want to see how that is reflected in the stock price. When you compare the cash flow to the stock price, you're assessing how much cash you get for the price you pay. It's a measure that's not unlike the price-to-earnings ratio, or P/E, where you assess how much earnings you get for the price of the stock. If a company has a lot of cash per share, it's a sure sign of an undervalued stock. A useful benchmark for the cash-to-price ratio is 10 to 1.

The higher the cash per share the more attractive the stock is. Remember a decade ago when corporate raiders targeted cash-rich companies for takeovers and then took the money and ran? Clearly, investors can benefit from high cash levels. Just ask Chrysler shareholders. The automaker's stock jumped handsomely after Kirk Kerkorian's celebrated takeover bid. And what made Chrysler so attractive to Kerkorian? Chrysler's huge cash reserve of $7.3 billion.

But beware as you read the cash flow statement. A company may show a big increase in cash flow from operations. But scan down the columns and check out the net increase or decrease in cash flow. Despite the increase from operations, the company could suffer a drop in its cash position because of spending on investments or financing. In some cases, that may be a warning flag; in others, it may not.

Making Sense of Book Value

This is a good point at which to say again that a decision on whether or not to buy a stock should never be based on a single criterion. You must weigh as many aspects as possible about a company and its financial condition in order to make a reasoned judgment about the prospects for its stock. Yet some money managers will have you believe that practically the only aspect worth considering is book value—the amount of a company's assets minus its liabilities. (You can find this figure for a company in *Value Line.*) While important, book value is only one measure of a stock's attractiveness. If your potential investment passes the book value test, do a little hip-hop and move on to the next test.

Determining whether a stock is a good buy from the book value angle is fairly simple. What you want is a company whose stock price is lower than its book value per share. For instance, if a stock is priced at $40 a share and its book value is $60 per share, you want to look more deeply into this potential investment. That's because the price of the stock is below the company's net worth.

Consider IBM. After its well-publicized troubles, its stock price plunged. But when the stock was selling at $45 a share, the company's book value was $68. That told some investors that maybe IBM stock wasn't really such a dog. Relying on book value as one important criterion, investors who bought IBM at $45 soon rediscovered their love of Big Blue. Not so long afterward, it was trading at $90.

But there's a catch. Determining a company's true book value can sometimes be quite tricky. Since book value basically is a company's assets minus its liabilities, you need to know the genuine value of those balance sheet items. But companies sometimes overstate their assets and understate their liabilities, thereby pumping up their book value.

For instance, suppose a dressmaker has a bunch of miniskirts in its warehouse and values them at $40 each. But miniskirts may be out of fashion, and in reality the company would be lucky to get $5 for each one. That company's book value is going to look a lot better than it truly is.

In essence, book value should translate into what a company would bring if it were broken up and each of its assets sold. For the dressmaker, that would mean selling not only the miniskirts but the machines that make them, the factory building itself, the land, the unused fabric, and so on. But if the value of the assets is inflated on the balance sheet, then the company will not realize the expected return on the breakup and individual sale of those assets.

It's pretty hard to know if a company actually *is* playing with the book value. There have been some notable surprises in true book value that left some investors with nasty wounds. But the measure is still used as a reasonably reliable window on a company's financial state.

The big proponents of book value even go so far as to say that many companies actually attempt through fancy accounting to understate book value. For tax reasons, companies prefer to deflate their assets and increase their liabilities, causing book value to shrink. For an investor, it's the best of all worlds to buy a company whose book value is higher than its stock price but below its true breakup value, which is what you'd get if you sold all the company's assets separately.

Book value isn't much use in measuring certain intangibles. For instance, everybody knows the Campbell's name. It's the soup America has grown up on for generations. Campbell's may have a terrific book value when you count its huge plant and product assets. But the company has something else that book value simply can't measure: brand-name recognition. Many people buy Campbell's soup simply because of product loyalty. It's an important aspect of a company's success but it's an intangible that doesn't show up on the balance sheet.

Where book value really falls short is as a measure of innovation. Book value is best for analyzing companies that have huge tangible assets, such as the steelmakers. For many other companies, especially those in technology, a real asset often is creativity. Book value tells you nothing about which companies will prove to be the true innovators in their industries. If I had relied only on book value to make stock market decisions, I never would have discovered two of my greatest picks: Chipcom and Corel. When I bought Chipcom it was selling at $54 a share, while its book value was about $10. Corel was trading at $8 a share, with a book value of $2.

Working Capital

No discussion of financial numbers would be complete without at least a mention of working capital. It deserves a look if for no other reason than its importance to Benjamin Graham's ideas on stock picking. In *The Intelligent Investor*, Graham calls working capital the "single criteria for choosing stocks."

Working capital is a company's current assets minus its total liabilities. Basically, working capital is what a company has available for day-to-day operations. Since it's best to look at this figure as it relates to the share price, you have to translate the total working capital into an amount per share. To get the per share figure, you divide the working capital by the number of the company's shares. Then compare the working capital per share to the stock's price per share. Graham advocated buying stocks that were selling at a price below working capital. That's the way to get excellent value in your investment.

It's a great idea but there are now drawbacks. In the first place, Graham influenced the investing strategies of so many market players that when a stock does sell below working capital hordes of investors jump in. That creates an unhealthy stampede mentality. Moreover, a stock that trades below working capital doesn't stay at that level for very long because of the intensity of buying.

As a result, there aren't many stocks these days that can be found selling at a price below working capital. Worse, it sometimes happens now that those companies that do fit the profile have some intrinsic problem that has knocked their stock price so low. Nonetheless, I think it's always a good idea to take note of the figure for working capital to share price. On a rare occasion, the figure might provide some special insight.

Price-to-Earnings Ratio

Of all the numbers to examine, probably the easiest to find is the price-to-earnings ratio. It's very useful and easy to understand.

You can find the number in almost any newspaper that carries stock tables. It's listed on the same line with the company's closing stock price, the high and low for the day, and so forth.

The ratio gives you a sense of the stock's price in relationship to the company's earnings. You arrive at it by dividing the stock price by the earnings per share. Consider Cincinnati Gas & Electric. Suppose its stock price is $22 a share and its earnings per share during the last twelve months were $2.24. Then its price-to-earnings ratio would be 9.8. Compare that to a technology company such as America Online, a leading provider of on-line information services for personal computers. Suppose its price is $75 and its earnings in the last twelve months were 76 cents a share. It would be trading at a P/E of 98.7.

The lower the P/E the better. The way I see it, P/E lets you know how much value you're getting for the price you pay for a stock. As with anything else, you don't want to overpay and you want to feel that what you bought is worth the price.

The standard view is that P/E measures the market's perception of a stock and its expectations of the stock's price movement. If Cincinnati Gas & Electric is trading at a P/E of 9.8, then it's fair to say the market doesn't expect much movement out of that stock. On the other hand, if America Online is trading at a P/E of 98.7, then the market expects that stock to perform.

Many investment professionals believe P/E also measures risk. The idea is that a high-P/E stock will rise *and* fall faster than a stock with a low-P/E. Of course, that implies that a low-P/E stock will rise more slowly and fall less precipitously than a high-P/E stock. I don't entirely agree.

Sure, a high-P/E stock will fall faster than a low-P/E stock. But a low-P/E stock may rise very fast, just as fast as a high-P/E stock. P/E doesn't measure everything about a company. Far from it. A low P/E doesn't necessarily mean the company is weak, just as a high P/E doesn't mean the company is strong. Good companies often fall into the low-P/E range simply because the market, for whatever reason, doesn't expect a lot of the company. In my view, it's more often the case that stocks are mispriced than priced correctly. And that's good news for smart investors who study the numbers carefully. Since the market doesn't expect much from a company selling for a low P/E, it doesn't take a lot of good news to get the stock price really moving. If you read the company's numbers correctly and foresee the good news coming, you're sitting on a gold mine. Similarly, a low-P/E stock isn't likely to be adversely affected by bad news since the market already is expecting the worst.

P/E does pose some problems for the investor. The ratios listed in the newspaper are based on earnings during the last twelve months. That figure is known as the trailing P/E, and it really reflects a historical picture of the company. That's a little troubling, because who's to say the future will be like the past?

In order to get around that question, many analysts work out estimates for future earnings. You can get a P/E based on future earnings called a forward P/E. But just as trailing P/Es may not enlighten you about the future, forward P/Es are little more than educated guesses about what a company's profits will be.

A *Forbes* study underscored the rather dismal ability of Wall Street analysts to predict company earnings. The study gave the analysts every possible opportunity to come up with their best estimates, even allowing them to adjust their forecasts a week before earnings were announced. Nevertheless, the analysts missed the mark by a wide margin: Their forecasts diverged from the actual earnings by an average 44%.

Even though that's a huge margin of error, I still don't believe investors should entirely ignore future earnings estimates. You can look at them as probabilities and use those probabilities to help you decide whether or not to buy a stock. Since several investment services evaluate many analysts' estimates, the services are able to provide the high, low, and average predictions for companies.

When calculating forward earnings, it's best to use the lowest profit forecasts. Doing this allows you to build a worst case profit scenario for your potential stock pick. If the numbers cause you concern at this point, then it's the right time to reject the stock. Remember studying P/Es is a great way to get excited about a stock, but it's also the way to jettison the dangerous ones before it's too late.

Earnings Growth

Since P/Es are largely based on earnings growth, it's important to discuss earnings in a little more depth. If there's one figure that investors must keep a very sharp eye on, it's a company's earnings. (Remember: Net income, net profit, and net earnings are synonymous.) It's a truism about stock investing that two engines basically drive the market: earnings and interest rates.

The level of interest rates helps determine the overall outlook for the market. In general, rising rates discourage stock market investors because other investments such as certificates of deposit begin to look more attractive. Higher rates bring higher returns on CDs and other bank deposits without the risk of fluctuation that is always present in the stock market. So money that would normally go into stocks is put instead into safer, higher-yielding investments.

Higher interest rates also have an impact on the other engine of the stock market: corporate earnings. It is a fact that high interest rates cause the economy to slow down. When rates are high, companies are discouraged from investing in new equipment for expansion, and consumers are reluctant to pay high monthly rates to finance a home or car. The result is that earnings slow down for companies that build cars, homes, and other products. Not only that, the ripple effects cause profits to deteriorate for companies that supply parts and services to the manufacturers. If you take the analysis a step further, you see that when home sales drop so does the home furnishings business, as well as sales of fabrics and other raw goods to make the furniture.

In a higher-interest-rate environment, many companies suffer declines in earnings growth. And that's not good for stocks, since good profits are crucial for driving a company's stock price up.

So investors must pay close attention to a company's earnings. As with P/Es there are two basic ways to look at earnings: backward and forward. A problem with past earnings is summed up in the phrase, "You can't be a very good driver if you constantly look in the rearview mirror." True enough, but I do see some advantages in studying past earnings. You can get a sense of where the company is coming from. The past performance gives you a picture of management's skills, the company's current value, and its general success.

Future earnings, as I said in the P/E section, are trickier to nail down. But I find that a practical way to assess the future is to look carefully at a company's products. Profits depend on the quality of what a company produces, so if you can assess the product itself you will have a solid idea of how profits may look in the future. Again, you must use the other criteria already mentioned in our discussion to size up the product and its likely impact on earnings.

So how much earnings growth is good? As far as I'm concerned, the higher the growth the better. Some people shy away from companies with rocket speed growth such as 40% a year or even 80%. They argue that the stock prices of companies that grow that fast are invariably too high. Not only that, they contend you may pay a lot and then the growth might slow and the price crash. The common view is that hot profit growth can't continue forever.

But I believe a company can't grow too fast. Suppose a dynamo software company has been piling up profit growth at a 60% rate a year for the past few years. Wouldn't you want to be invested in a company like that? The pessimists would say, "But that kind of growth is unsustainable!" I couldn't agree more. However, even if growth slowed to 30%, the company's profit picture would still outshine most others. Sure, its stock price would probably drop, but provided the company meets our other financial criteria, it remains an attractive investment. The lower stock price will only create a tempting opportunity to buy more in anticipation of another run-up and will lower the overall cost of your shares.

Let me put it another way: You can never have a company that grows too fast—just as you can never have a basketball player who's too tall. People often worry about companies that grow too fast; they point to some of the problems of speedy growth such as high stock price and overwhelming debt. But to my mind, it's not the fast growth that's the problem: It's the associated problems such growth brings. It's the same with tall basketball players. People always criticize a player who's seven and a half feet tall for being slow, or a poor ball handler, or just plain uncoordinated. All that may be true. But the problem isn't the guy's size: It's the associated problems.

So what do you do? You seek out fast-growing companies that aren't experiencing the ill effects of their growth. Two examples come to mind: In their early stages, both Microsoft and Novell demonstrated super growth without the negative side effects. Similarly, you look for the giants on the basketball court who can run and pass smoothly. Then their height is an incredible asset, not a liability. We have to look no further than Wilt Chamberlain and Kareem Abdul-Jabbar.

I'd be less than honest, however, if I didn't point out that sometimes the only way to find companies without the defects is to lower your requirements for profit growth. Maybe a little less growth is okay, say 20% a year, just as a little less height in a basketball player can be fine. Michael Jordan may not be seven and a half feet tall, but who wouldn't want him on his team?

Price-to-Research Ratio

If you're looking for strong technology stocks, one aspect you must analyze closely is the company's commitment to research and development. No terrific breakthroughs or fantastic new products occur without healthy funding for R & D. But how do you measure whether a company is devoting enough money to this critical area?

In a fascinating and original book, *Super Stocks: The Book That's Changing the Way Investors Think on Wall Street,* Kenneth Fisher provides an answer. Fisher, who has a regular column in *Forbes,* introduced a concept called the price-to-research ratio. It's a number that the wise investor should certainly study before deciding to buy a technology stock.

But as Fisher points out, the ratio is a valuable yardstick only when all the other criteria check out favorably. You don't want to buy a stock just because it has an attractive price-to-research ratio; but an attractive ratio along with other positive aspects will help you lean toward taking the plunge.

A company's research funding isn't as easy to find as many other numbers. But you can often find it in a company's annual report or in its 10-K filing with the Securities and Exchange Commission. Both these documents are usually available from the library or the company itself. You should look for whatever amount is stated as the research budget. Besides the company's money devoted to research, this number should also include any outside R & D funding, either from the government or other third parties. To arrive at the ratio, you total up the figures and divide the sum by the company's market value, which is the company's share price multiplied by the number of shares outstanding.

Analyzing the ratio helps you determine whether the stock is decently priced relative to the level of the company's research funding. Fisher recommends that investors never buy a stock that has a price-to-research ratio of more than 15. You should be very happy, Fisher says, to find a stock with a ratio between 5 and 10.

Short Interest

If a stock checks out well in most other ways, a high level of short interest can add a gleam to an investor's eye. Short interest is the total number of shares that have been sold short but haven't been repurchased to close out those positions. Short interest gives you a picture of how many people think a stock will decline in price. It is based on short selling—a trading strategy in which market players borrow stock and sell it at a certain price in the expectation of repurchasing it later at a lower price. A look at short interest reveals how many shares of a company's stock are held short by investors.

You probably wonder, why in the world you would want to buy a stock that a lot of people are betting will sink? The answer is that the way things work on Wall Street, any time people get really pessimistic about a specific stock or the market as a whole, it's usually a good sign of an imminent rise in prices. This is the so-called contrarian view of investing. And there's quite a bit of logic to it.

If everyone thinks a stock is heading down, the reasoning goes, then probably most people who are going to sell have already sold. The price is already low and therefore may be attractive. So there's nowhere for the price to go but up. Likewise, if everyone thinks a stock is going up, then a huge number of people have probably bought the stock already. That doesn't leave a lot of money around for further investment in the stock. Moreover, the buying has already driven up the price so that a good number of investors may want to get their profit and run. The result: They sell and the price comes down.

High short interest is good for other reasons, too. Suppose a stock with considerable short interest begins to rise in price. Investors holding short positions will eventually lose their stomach and bail out. In order to do so, they must purchase shares, thereby driving prices even higher.

Even if the short seller gets it right, the price decline won't likely prove disastrous for owners of the stock. That's because as the price slumps many short sellers will be satisfied and take their profits. And again, the way they do that is by *buying* the stock, inevitably pushing the price up once more.

I must stress, however, short interest should never be used as a primary consideration in whether to buy a stock. It's just icing if everything else looks good. And if short interest isn't high, that shouldn't deter you from buying a promising stock.

Dividend Yield

Many investors buy stocks in large measure for their dividends. Companies that pay good, regular dividends provide a stream of income for investors above and beyond any appreciation in the stock price.

So many investors want to know the dividend payout of companies that the figure is among the most common numbers published. You can usually find the annual rate per share in your local newspaper next to the stock's closing price. To figure out the dividend yield, you divide the dividend by the stock price. What you get is a percentage figure that tells you how much income you're earning on your investment dollar.

For instance, suppose Exxon is trading at 70¾ and its dividend is $3 per share. Its dividend yield works out to 4.2%. So just for owning Exxon shares you're making 4.2% on your money. If the stock price climbs, then your total return would be even better when you sold your shares.

Sounds great, but I don't normally buy stocks for their dividend yields. For one thing, dividends are far from secure. Your yield from dividends should not be confused with something as certain as the yield on a certificate of deposit or a savings account. In good times, dividend yields may be even better as companies boost payouts. But just the same, companies may cut dividends, or fail to distribute them at all, in the bad times.

Most of the companies I buy don't usually distribute dividends, and if they do, the payouts are pretty skimpy. Instead, I prefer companies that keep their dividend payments for themselves to devote to expansion or research and development. If a company pays dividends, it usually diminishes the funds available to spur further growth. As we've seen, terrific gains in share prices come mostly from consistent, strong earnings growth.

However, decent dividends can serve as a cushion for your stock portfolio. Suppose you own a high dividend stock that comes under pressure and starts declining. As the share price falls, the dividend yield rises. So the income you get from the stock looks good, even though on paper the stock's value has slipped.

Adding It Up

By now your head is probably swimming with all the phrases I've discussed. Cash flow, book value, P/E ratios, short interest, and all the rest. Putting them together to make sound investment decisions may seem daunting. You'll see, though, that the process is simple.

The key now is to think of the numbers in relation to each other. Suppose your potential stock pick is a company that has great earnings growth but is a little weak in cash flow. Or what if profits seem to be slowing down a bit but the company's debt level has shrunk tremendously? You have to weigh one number against another, and use your best judgment to make the big decision whether or not to buy the stock. I want to offer some basic guidelines here to help you think through this last, crucial stage.

I've played a lot of team sports: basketball, baseball, soccer. And I've heard a lot of clichés about what makes a great team. The overriding theme of these clichés is that a team that pulls together—no matter how good or bad its individual players—comes out pretty well in the end. In other words, your team doesn't have to be packed with stars to win games.

I keep this notion in mind when I assess the numbers of a company whose stock I might buy. Think of a winning basketball team. It has twelve players. But not all of them have to be great to capture the championship. Really, only five need to be terrific; three or four can be pretty good, and the other three or four may never have played basketball before in their lives and can just sit on the bench all the time.

So it is with a company's numbers. Not every number has to be fabulous. Consider technology stocks, for instance. Strong earnings are very important when you consider an investment in technology. At the same time, stellar book value isn't an absolute necessity because book value doesn't take into account any intangible factors such as a great reputation or superior products. It also doesn't tell you anything about the great potential of some growth companies.

Of course, it would be wonderful to have all the numbers look great, just as it would be awesome to have all twelve basketball teammates score like Michael Jordan. That's simply unrealistic. By the same token, Jordan's great, but one standout doesn't carry a team, just as one great number doesn't carry a stock. Michael Jordan didn't start winning championship rings until at least a few of his supporting cast turned in strong performances.

To make a sound decision on whether to buy a stock, I use a two-part analysis of the numbers. The first part involves studying the numbers that measure the quality of the stock. After I decide the quality is good, I look at the numbers that tell me whether the stock is worth the price.

In assessing the quality of the company, I'm really looking for reasons to reject the stock. It's as important to know when to bid a hunch farewell as it is to know when to buy. My quality check involves a careful look at such numbers as the company's debt level, inventories, and profit growth. If a stock raises real concern on these criteria, I abandon any further thought about it. The hunch gets tossed.

Evaluating stocks at this stage is similar to my mother and sister's approach to buying a formal dress. Once they identify a potential purchase, they give it a thorough quality check without even caring about the price. The dress must have no serious defects.

More often than not, both the dress and the stock should pass this stage with flying colors. In both cases, you're initially looking for a well-made dress or a solid company, so it stands to reason you're not going to pick out a completely ratty dress or stock.

Key to a company's quality is its profitability. One area that gives a hint of future profits is the cash flow. It's best if cash flow per share is two or more times the level of earnings per share. For example, in 1985, the publisher Houghton Mifflin Company had a total cash flow of $38.7 million and earnings of $18.9 million. The cash-flow-to-net-income ratio was more than 2 to 1, which was quite attractive.

In further assessing a company's profitability, I take a close look at the return on equity. This figure, expressed as a percentage, tells a lot about how well the company manages shareholders' money. You want a high return on equity, in the neighborhood of 35% or more if you can. If the figure is 15% or lower, you'd do well to look for another stock.

Return on equity, available in *Standard & Poor's Stock Reports,* is very important because it gives a broad overview of a company's profitability. It shows how much profit a company delivers relative to the shareholders' equity, which is the value of the company in shareholders' hands. The number is derived in a variety of ways, depending on what source you consult. Generally, you simply divide the company's net profit by its shareholders' equity. For example, in 1989, consumer electronics retailer Circuit City had a net profit of $60 million and shareholders' equity of $230 million. The return on equity was 26%. Benjamin Graham in *Security Analysis* arrives at the number by a more complicated means. And Barron's *Dictionary of Finance and Investment Terms* says the figure is "calculated by dividing common stock equity at the beginning of the accounting period into net income for the period after preferred stock dividends but before common stock dividends."

Whatever calculation you use, it will work out pretty much the same as any other. Keep in mind that you want return on equity to be in the range of 10% to 15%. To put the company's profits in context, it's a good idea to check out the return on equity over several years. Beware that a company can raise its return on equity by boosting its debt-to-equity level. If you sense this is the reason behind a glowing return on equity, think again about that stock. It means the debt level has risen, which is never good, and I think throws a bit of a dark cloud over management.

The Final Step

After completing your quality check, it's time to grit your teeth and decide whether or not to buy the stock. Now you focus all your attention on the stock price. Just as my sister and mom ask themselves whether a formal dress is worth the price, I pose exactly the same question about my stocks. The question boils down to this:

Are you getting as much company and profitability as you should for the price you're paying?

For a value investor, this is indeed the most important question. After all, the value investor's aim is to buy stocks that haven't yet reached their true value. If the value investor buys an overvalued stock he risks owning an investment that will depreciate to its real value. On the other hand, if he reads the numbers correctly and buys a truly undervalued stock, he will reap the rewards as the market brings that stock's price up to its legitimate level.

To assess the price level of a stock, you need to consider the price-to-earnings ratio, cash flow to price, book value, dividend yield, and research to price.

Besides those numbers, there are a few handy formulas for assessing the level of a stock's price. One formula, introduced by Peter Lynch in *One Up on Wall Street*, offers a nifty way to know whether you're paying a decent price for the amount of growth and dividends a company provides. It's fairly simple: All you do is add the long-term growth rate to the dividend yield and divide by the price-to-earnings ratio. If you come up with less than 1, Lynch says, the stock is selling at a bad price. He adds that "1.5 is okay, but what you're really looking for is a 2 or better." The long-term growth rate is the average rate at which a company's earnings have grown over at least three years.

Consider Cedar Fair Limited Partnership, which operates amusement parks. In 1994, its profits were growing at an annual rate of 17.57%, its dividend yield was 7.7%, and its P/E ratio was 10.4. The arithmetic looks like this:

$$\frac{17.57 \text{ (growth rate)} + 7.7 \text{ (dividend yield)}}{10.4 \text{ (P/E ratio)}}$$

And the result is a quite attractive 2.4.

Another formula to keep in mind was suggested by Benjamin Graham in *Intelligent Investor*. He argues that a stock's price-to-earnings ratio should not be higher than 15 and that the current price should be no more than 1.5 times book value. Of course, it's difficult to arrive precisely at these figures, so Graham allows for variations in those numbers—but only within a range. If the stock is selling at a price-to-earnings ratio that's higher than 15, then its price must be lower than 1.5 times book value. Overall, the relationship between the two figures should remain constant, however. That is, together the multiple of the price-to-earnings ratio and book value shouldn't exceed 22.5. (That figure is achieved by multiplying the price-to-earnings ratio of 15 by the price of 1.5 times book value: $15 \times 1.5 = 22.5$.)

For instance, Travelers Inc. was trading at 1.42 times its book value in September 1994. Its price-to-earnings ratio was 8.7. The price-to-earnings and book value multiplied is 12.354, well below the 22.5 level deemed appropriate.

Finally, it's important to distinguish between growth investors and value investors. These different players look for different qualities in their stocks. Growth investors want stocks that are likely to produce exceptionally strong earnings; they're usually willing to pay a little more for that growth. Value investors, as we mentioned earlier, are interested in finding stocks that are undervalued. It should be pointed out, however, that the smart growth investor also keeps his eye out for those stocks that offer a tremendous amount of value for the price. All stocks—whether value or growth—must pass the quality check before being considered in terms of their price.

Important numbers to study for growth stocks include the growth rate, the price-to-research ratio (especially for technology stocks), and the price-to-earnings ratio. You also want to look at the price to cash flow, but keep in mind that the pure profitability ratios are more important. In addition, you must apply Lynch's formula mentioned above to your growth stock pick; it was designed specifically with growth stocks in mind.

Value stocks should be measured against all of the same numbers, with the exception of the Lynch formula. Not only that, they should have an especially strong showing in at least one of the numbers and at worst a mediocre reading for all the rest. A low price-to-earnings ratio is generally key, as long as the other numbers check out. Remember, a super-undervalued stock will jump out at you with many great numbers. But just like the championship basketball team, you can still win with a few stars.

What I find most gratifying about my approach to a company's numbers is that it decreases the chances of a major foul-up. My process may miss a few of the gigantic winners but it will catch a lot of them. Just as important, though, it will raise red flags over the potential losers and take them out of consideration. Never forget: Rejecting a dog stock at the outset is as valuable to the long-term performance of your portfolio as picking a winner.

CHAPTER EIGHT

Miss a Market Rally?
No Big Deal

An Ocean of Stocks

People blabber endlessly about what The Market is doing. Is it a good market? A bad market? Has the market reached its high? Or is it at a low? Frankly, it doesn't really matter. All the discussion of market trends only matters to people investing in the short term. If you're a long-term investor, as you should be, what the market is doing now, or in the next few weeks or few months is hardly worth worrying about.

I'll go even further and say you shouldn't even have to give the overall market a thought if you invest according to my approach. In the language of Wall Street, my style is called the bottom-up method. It simply means, as you've seen in this book, that I focus on the strengths of individual companies and pay less attention to the ebb and flow of the overall stock market.

Of course, many investors choose to ride the currents. They take the big picture view, analyzing the direction of the economy and interest rates and then buying stocks they think will benefit from the trends. These brave souls are known as top-down investors.

The top-down style is popular among big mutual fund managers. These professional money managers are hamstrung by a ton of rules governing what they can invest in and how much they can buy of an individual company. Often they have so much money to invest that they have to find a lot of companies with good prospects. For them, an effective and easy way to do that is to survey the economic landscape with a top-down perspective and buy the stocks that are best positioned to benefit from likely trends. In this way, they can do a broad sweep of the market and reel in many companies at once.

I don't reject top-down investing out of hand. I think both the top-down and the bottom-up methods are effective. I find it's easier to zero in on great companies and ignore all the noise in the market.

To me, the overall stock market is like the ocean—big and deep and ultimately unfathomable. So why waste time trying to guess which way the massive currents will flow? Get yourself a sturdy oceangoing vessel and don't worry about the swells that await you.

In other words, buy solid stocks, just as you'd choose an aircraft carrier over a rowboat to cross the Pacific Ocean.

Don't get me wrong: Sure, the overall market has an impact on individual stocks, just as the currents rock an aircraft carrier. But the truth is, the impact is far overrated, especially for long-term investors. It's a myth that market trends determine the success of your portfolio.

A successful ocean crossing depends a lot more on the type of vessel than on the currents themselves. Even though there's the odd chance that a favorable current will carry a rowboat safely across the Pacific, I'd much rather lay my money on the aircraft carrier. The big ship will survive the crossing virtually every time, and the ocean's swells will have only a minimal impact on it.

It's much easier picking the right boat for the journey than predicting how the ocean will behave.

Scary World of Prediction

The whole realm of stock market prediction frightens me. Timing the market, which is in essence forecasting its direction, is among the hardest things in life. I would admire anyone who could master it. So far, nobody has been able to predict the market with any real long-term success. To forecast movements of the overall market, you have to evaluate a gargantuan amount of information—everything from the reams of government economic statistics to the Federal Reserve's thinking on interest rates. You even have to factor in unforeseen events such as the Gulf War. But if the event is unforeseen, how the heck are you supposed to evaluate it? So now I hope the mammoth task of market prediction is more apparent to you.

Nonetheless, market professionals, analysts, and economists still constantly spout their predictions. When they get lucky, they become stars. When they get it wrong, nobody pays attention. If you consistently read *The Wall Street Journal*, you can't help noticing how often the pundits revise their forecasts. One day, interest rates are headed lower, everybody says. The next day, they're headed the opposite direction, the same people say.

The market is made up of so many different components that predicting the overall market is something of a joke. Even if you're roughly right about the economic trends, how do you know for sure how those trends will affect all stocks? Stocks with big capitalizations respond differently from stocks with small capitalizations. Stocks within one industry are sensitive to factors that have no impact on another industry.

The Wall Street pros try to get around all the subtleties by focusing on the well known indexes as measures of the entire market. People mistakenly equate the trends in the Standard & Poor's 500-stock index and the Dow Jones Industrial Index to the trend of the overall market. I don't buy it. Though those indexes do represent a good portion of the market, they really don't come close to encompassing the whole market. They really only cover the stocks of large companies that are often most affected by cycles in the economy. There are other huge regions of the market, including stocks of midsize companies and, even more important in some respects, small-cap stocks. When the professionals refer to The Market, they should be more careful with their language.

To ascribe a certain trend to the whole market based on a few stocks is the same as stereotyping a group of people based on a few individuals. I like to think of myself as color-blind; I look at everybody the same way regardless of race, religion, or color. Not only that, I think that anybody who doesn't look at others in that way misses much of the variety and beauty of life.

So it is with the stock market, too. It's a huge multifaceted culture, in essence, made up of many different individuals. Once you start stereotyping the market as all good or all bad based on a few stocks in the indexes, you're bound to miss many of the hidden jewels. Dig a little below the indexes and you'll discover the true heartbeat of the market.

The Market Doesn't Exist

I personally don't pay much attention to the S&P 500 or the Dow industrials. For me, the market that those indexes represent simply doesn't exist. Sure, they jump around in the short term, reflecting the level of nervousness or enthusiasm in the market. But over the long term, the indexes don't mean much to your individual stocks; your stocks will move on the basis of your companies' own successes. I think all the attention heaped on the market indexes belittles the overwhelming importance of individual stocks.

Remember, buying stock is the same as buying a piece of a company. If you have a good company, or a good stock, it'll be good no matter what's going on in the market. Resist the temptation to accept the mumbo jumbo that flies around in the market. Keep your head—and stick to your sound approach—in the face of such comments as: "This is such a terrible market that my worst enemy shouldn't be invested!" or "This is such a great market I'm putting every penny I have into it!"

These sentiments tend to crop up around market highs and lows. Of course, it's impossible to know where market highs or lows really are until after the fact. Nevertheless, people are always talking about them, always predicting them.

To cut through all the bull, I use a simple approach in dealing with questions about market highs and lows. You can tell if the market is high, or near a high, by how difficult it is to find good undervalued stocks. An overheated market tends to push stock prices up beyond their reasonable value, so it's tough to come up with solid, cheap stocks. A market high may be signalled by the beginning of a pattern of declines among the overvalued stocks. There always comes a point when an overvalued stock must readjust to its correct value.

Conversely, you can tell if the market is low, or near a low, by the number of good undervalued stocks lying around. A market that's been beaten up tends to knock stocks below their true value. If undervalued stocks start gaining in price, it's a reasonable assumption that the market low has been hit and a rally is in the offing.

Oops, now I'm giving advice on how to predict the market. I'll stop right there. But my blunder underscores a point about predictions: Despite all I've said about the impossibility of getting it right, you always fall into the trap of trying. I myself get asked all the time to offer my forecast of the market. Right after people ask, "Got any stock tips?" they want to know, "So what's going to happen to the overall market?"

I've devised a way to handle these inquiries. You're free to use them yourself, if you like, after you attract a little attention for your smart stock picks.

In the first place, I always keep in mind that nobody ever gets it right. In the second place, people may ask for your predictions but they often don't use them anyway. They forget what you said as soon as they move on to the next conversation. I suppose someone may run out and buy stock index futures based on my market forecast, but it's not very likely. What's worse, someone may run back to his full-service broker and ask him about my prediction. Then the broker will explain that he's the true professional and ramble on with his own advice. And who knows what harm will befall the listener's portfolio?

Now, for the sake of argument, suppose the inquirer actually remembers my prediction. Under such circumstances, it's good to have a few safe guidelines. Remember, people asking about the direction of the market aren't concerned with next year or the year after that. They want to know what's going to happen in the next few weeks or months. Given that, I'd never stick my neck out foolishly and say, "Well, of course, the Dow will slide from 4000 to 200 in the next four months."

The point is, I avoid being too specific in my predictions. It's completely ridiculous to make specific predictions, and if you are ever encouraged to listen to any, my advice is to excuse yourself graciously and walk away. Who in their right mind would ever have any faith in someone forecasting that the S&P 500 will close at

625.48 next Tuesday? If someone told you that, and the index did actually comply, all you can do is laugh at the coincidence.

When I'm really pushed into a corner for a prediction, all I can do is rely on what I call the Gut Indicator. I've examined many prediction systems, and believe me, none is as accurate as this one. That's not to say it actually works. But it's as close as I've come to a way of reading the tea leaves. Of course, its effectiveness will vary among different people.

The Gut Indicator simply calls upon your instincts about current economic conditions. I've found that most people have a better sense about the economy than they give themselves credit for. They may not be able to translate it into graphs and fancy equations, but they feel the direction in which things are generally drifting. I like to use my gut feelings about the economy in predicting the market simply because the market usually leads the economic trend. So if you think the economy will pick up in a few months, you can tell people you think the market will do okay over the next few weeks.

When coming up with a prediction, I ask my gut for its opinion on everything I've read recently, noticed in my community, and heard from people I've encountered. I also try to assess my feeling about the momentum in the economy. How strong is it? Is it slowing down? These are indications of how the market will perform.

The Gut Indicator may not be foolproof. But at least it comes directly from your own soul. No one else will have the same gut level reactions to the world around you.

And if your prediction turns out to be wrong, so what! Join the crowd. You have the advantage of knowing you don't rely on overall market predictions, because you follow the bottom-up approach in selecting seaworthy stocks that stay afloat no matter how rough the waters.

Have I Got a Stock for You!

A Warning About Investment Advice

Choosing a Broker

Now that you've studied your stock picks carefully, weeding out the dogs and zeroing in on the potential winners, how do you go about actually purchasing your stocks? Choosing a broker is an important step in the investment process.

You have two choices: a full-service broker or a discount broker. The full-service broker caters to the client's needs. He will recommend stocks, set up a financial plan, execute trades. He'll sell you not only stocks but also bonds, certificates of deposit, mutual funds, and sometimes even tax shelters. For all this full service, you pay full commission. Your full-service broker will cost you two to three times as much as a discount broker. Full-service brokerage firms include Merrill Lynch and PaineWebber.

The discount broker, by contrast, merely executes trades. Originally established as barebones operations, discount brokers often don't offer much else in the way of service. The benefit is that you save a lot of money. Lately, however, some discount brokers have been adding various types of services to their operations. At Schwab, as I mentioned earlier, you can use the brokerage's resources to research stocks. Fidelity also has a discount operation that provides some useful services. The type and quality of services at discount brokers varies with the firms. I rank Schwab and Fidelity at the top in the services they provide to discount customers. Other firms offer lower fees but also fewer services.

I chose a discount broker when I first started investing. There were a couple of reasons. I didn't have much money to invest and wanted to use as much as possible for actual investments rather than commission fees. Not only that, I knew exactly what I was going to buy and I didn't think I needed any advice. To tell the truth, I was also a cheapskate.

I chose Schwab over Fidelity for practical reasons. Both were fairly far from my house. But Schwab was in Troy, while Fidelity was in the next city. Since they were very competitive in their services and costs, Schwab got my business because of its location.

I reject full-service brokers because they spend a lot of time pushing stocks on you. They try to get you to buy stocks you might otherwise not ever consider. That may be good on the odd chance a broker really has a sharp recommendation. But more often than not, the full-service broker is just trying to get you to trade. That's how he makes his money—from the commissions on your account.

Don't get me wrong: There are lots of good, trustworthy brokers. But I don't approve of the commission system under which they work. While you're trying to make money by buying good stocks, the full-service broker makes money no matter how well your stocks perform, if he sells them to you. If you buy his advice and make a lot of trades with him, you help finance his kid's college education—while your own kids go begging because of all the money you spent on commissions.

Full-service brokers, however, can be useful simply for all the information they provide. Aside from recommending stocks, they're supposed to give you whatever data and analysis you might need to make your own decisions. It's all part of the hefty commission fees.

Which type of broker you choose depends a lot on your own style and financial means. If you like doing your own company research in the library, as I do, and have your own strong views on what stocks to buy, a discount broker is probably your best bet. If you have more money at your disposal for helpful services and prefer the input of others, then you'd probably like working with a full-service broker. It all comes down to where you feel the most comfortable and how much you're willing to pay for the services you receive.

Gurus Everywhere

Some people pay big bucks for fancy investment advice. But you don't have to pay a lot for it. It's everywhere.

Flip on the TV. There's CNBC correspondent Dan Dorfman spouting off about one stock or another. His ability to move stocks is becoming legendary. He's often right about the companies he targets for discussion. In May 1995, he reported that Bradlees Inc. was likely to file for bankruptcy. The stock plunged. In June, the company sought Chapter 11 protection.

In July 1995, Dorfman reported that Westinghouse Electric Corporation was planning to buy CBS, sending CBS shares up 6%. It wasn't until the next day that *The New York Times* and *The Wall Street Journal* had the story.

Dorfman is far from alone among the investment talking heads on TV. Every Friday, you find the roundtable folks of Louis Rukeyser's *Wall Street Week* rattling off their stock picks for the week.

You can also get recommendations from CNN's *MoneyLine* with Lou Dobbs. Almost always whenever anybody associated with Wall Street shows up on TV, you're bound to hear a stock or two singled out for praise.

TV doesn't have the monopoly on stock advice. Check out your local newsstand. The number of investment magazines these days is mindboggling. It's not enough that Fidelity runs a huge mutual fund company; now it publishes quite a sophisticated personal finance magazine called *Worth Financial Intelligence.* Even *The Wall Street Journal* isn't content to be the top business newspaper in the country. Now it, too, publishes a sharp personal finance magazine called *SmartMoney*, in conjunction with Hearst.

These publications are only the latest in a crowded field that includes such old standbys as *Money* and *Kiplinger's Personal Finance Magazine.* And of course, the major business magazines such as *Fortune* and *Forbes* also have stock columns where the latest hot picks are featured.

Indeed, investment advice is one of the hottest areas in the media. Many city newspapers have expanded their business pages to offer words of wisdom to stock market players. Even *The New York Times* undertook a major revamping of its business section. One major result, as far as I can tell, is that the Sunday business page is now a repository of helpful hints for anyone with money. Regular features offer guidance on how to earn, spend, and invest money.

This media mania wouldn't happen if people didn't want investment advice. I'm probably the least likely person to run out and buy a stock because someone recommends it in the media. But I confess I do find myself at least listening to what people are pushing. It's simply one of my three principles: Educate yourself.

I do think one type of advice is especially worthwhile. For obvious reasons, I find it very difficult to speak ill of investment guide books. Reading investment books is one of my favorite hobbies. It's been a while since I read fiction, as I'm so absorbed by investment studies of all kinds. As with stock recommendations, it's important not to be brainwashed by any single investment book. Think of them all as offering a fine buffet. Pick and choose what you like, and leave the rest.

Takeover Trauma

Many stock recommendations these days center on takeover rumors. This type of rumor has been popular practically ever since stocks were first traded. But the popular media—especially movies like *Wall Street* and the book and movie *Barbarians at the Gate*—helped dupe the public into believing it's easy to make a killing from a takeover.

Sure, a lot of investors have managed to make a bundle in a short time. A takeover, or the rumor of one, works magic on a stock price. Often, the takeover company is willing to pay more than the current stock price to acquire the company, causing the shares to rise. Sometimes a takeover offer initiates a bidding war that drives the stock price up even higher. Some investors end up smiling from ear to ear. Ask anyone holding Lotus stock when IBM decided to gobble up the company. Or what about shareholders of Capital Cities/ABC? That stock shot up more than $22 after Disney announced plans to buy the company.

But just as some people win, there are a lot of people out there still licking their wounds from some sure bet on a takeover. You probably don't want to bring up the subject to anybody who bought Hilton Hotels following its takeover rumors. The stock climbed in anticipation of an announcement. But no announcement ever came, causing the stock eventually to crumble. Anyone who didn't get out in time got burned. Amid the rumors Hilton had climbed as high as $115 a share only to sink again to $34.

The takeover arena attracts suckers. They're drawn in by the fast pace, the overwhelming excitement, and of course, the whiff of a fortune. I can't stress enough: Be careful! It's all right to listen to takeover rumors and even to chase after the stocks. But you really should have some ground rules.

First and foremost, cut your chances of a disaster by chasing stocks only of companies that would seem great anyway, even without the takeover rumor. That means the stock should be able to pass the tests we put potential investments through in this book. If the target is a good stock anyway and the takeover deal fails to pan out, there's still hope for your long-term investment.

Another useful ground rule is to stop and ask yourself: Why would the aggressor in the deal want the takeover company? If you can't come up with a watertight argument, keep your wallet shut.

It's easy to get suckered into believing a sure bet takeover rumor. Everybody—regardless of position—always keeps an ear open for that one great idea that will make him rich. And we listen all the more closely if the font of wisdom happens to be an authoritative-looking person in a natty outfit—in other words, an old guy with white hair sporting a $1,500 suit.

Power of TV

We're suckers for advice because we've been trained since childhood to respect authority. Someone who looks right and tells you something that seems reasonable must be right. That, at least, is pretty much how our minds work, and it's scary. What's worse, we accept the advice—especially the blabber on TV—because we assume that everyone else accepts it, too. For many people, there's nothing more comforting than following the crowd. The irony is that while the stock tip is dished up as if it were just for you alone, it's really being broadcast for the entire world. You think you're getting some great secret knowledge, but at the same time you're overjoyed to think that so many other people will be thinking exactly like you after hearing the advice. Jump on the bandwagon, you're thinking, because now the stock has to go up. And that mentality is precisely what drives many people to call their brokers immediately.

The unfortunate part is that people just don't use their heads. They hear a recommendation—any kind of recommendation—and they don't do the necessary work to investigate it. They just accept the advice at face value. That's a sure road to the poor house.

I'm not saying that you should reject all investment advice out of hand. Not all recommendations are bad. The important thing is to make sure you stay clear-headed. People want so much to believe in the Wall Street pundits that they surrender their own brains to them. If there is one sound bit of advice about investment advice, it's this: Don't let it blur your vision.

I wouldn't want you to accept my own stock recommendations blindly. On occasion, after great insistence, I have given in to demands for advice. I've given recommendations to individuals. Even worse, I've coughed up stock picks to a large general audience on national television. I've always regretted doing it.

A Moral Question

Recommending stocks to the public at large is much worse in a moral sense than recommending to an individual. At least with an individual such as a friend, you have the chance to revise your advice when you see the person again.

In my brief career I've had the misfortune of recommending three stocks to the general public. Each time, my stock picks happened to behave rather erratically and probably gave a case of the terrors to whoever followed my advice. But in the long run, the picks proved pretty good.

My first recommendation was made at 5:19 P.M. on March 8, 1994. It was the day *The Wall Street Journal* put me on the front page, and I was inundated with calls from the media in the United States and around the world. That evening I agreed to do a live interview at home with a local TV news station.

I was caught completely off guard when the interviewer suddenly popped the question, "So, Matt, give us your sure thing."

Man, was I on the spot!

I tried to wriggle out of it. I explained that there are no sure things in the investment world. But clearly the interviewer wasn't satisfied. I felt the pressure building.

I blurted out, "Chipcom."

The interviewer said, "Great. I'll call my broker right after the show and tell him to buy 100 shares."

I had that sinking feeling in my stomach. My God, this guy was going to follow my advice. Who knows how many others out there would do the same thing?

It was as if I'd crossed some imaginary line. The door had opened a crack and I stumbled over the threshold. There was no going back.

Even though I felt troubled about offering advice, I wound up recommending the stock again and again over the next few weeks. Whether in newspaper interviews or on radio talk shows or TV, the word Chipcom kept popping out of my mouth.

The day after I first recommended Chipcom, the stock jumped from $37 to $40. I wasn't big-headed enough yet to think the gain was due to me and my mouth. Besides, there were clearly some news events and other factors that played into a short-term rise.

Nevertheless some people were impressed. A girl at my high school told me her cousin bought Chipcom right after I had touted it. He was happy because he rode it up to $40 and made some money. She now wanted to know if I had any other hot tips. I politely told her no, I did not.

One of the regulars at Schwab informed me that he was now the proud owner of 400 shares of Chipcom. Rather than worrying, I began to feel pretty good. If all these people were buying stocks based on my advice, well, I figured my advice mustn't have been *that* bad. Clearly, my emotions were overrunning my logic.

The flattery didn't last. After hovering around $40 for a short time, the stock began tumbling. In five months, Chipcom was selling at $21. That was an ugly 47% decline.

Boy, did I feel bad. Not so much for myself. I was confident it was a good stock and would come bouncing back. But how many of those people who put their blind faith in me would have the stomach to hold on?

Chipcom did eventually rebound. Over the next seven months, it went from $21 to $50.

I offered my second recommendation about two months later when I appeared on *The Phil Donahue Show*. Near the end of the show somebody in the audience pushed me over the line again. She asked, "What stocks are you recommending?"

I was reluctant. But still I blurted out a recommendation: Best Buy, I said, was a good stock at that time.

When the show was taped in May 1994, Best Buy was trading at around $29. The show didn't air until July 22, and by that time the stock had plunged to $23. After the broadcast, the stock fell a little more. Again, I wasn't proving any kind of immediate wizard.

But then the advice proved sound. After its initial decline, the stock revived in a major way and climbed to $45 a share over the next few months.

My third recommendation came in early 1995 when *The Wall Street Journal* published a follow-up article about me. My choice this time was a small stock called Cott Corporation. It's a Canadian private label soft drink maker. It also is the leading manufacturer of private label canned pet foods. The company is licenser and distributor of R. C. Cola and Rite in parts of Canada, and uses R. C. Cola's formula in its own premium colas. Cott produces Sainsbury Cola for Sainsbury grocery stores in Britain, Sam's American Choice for Wal-Mart, and Safeway Select for the Safeway stores.

By the time I found it, the stock had lost its fizz. It was down more than 70% to $10.38 from its high of $37.80. I was confident the stock had fallen far too much. Given the strength of the company, the stock was poised to take off again. In the back of my mind, I kept recalling reports I'd seen saying that in mass market taste tests, people actually preferred the Cott cola to the major brands.

So I opened my big mouth again. The day I recommended the stock, it inched up 25 cents to $10.60. After that, it was downhill. Cott slid 25% to $8. It stayed there for a while as though purposely reddening my face.

Then the turnaround came, and Cott recovered and climbed to $13 within a few months.

Still, this is the best advice I can give: Do your own homework on any tips you pick up.

Bailing Out Too Soon

What all this tells you is that you must hold on to good companies, no matter what happens in the short term. But more important, I hope you'll understand from my public stock pronouncements that you should never accept recommendations at face value. People who didn't really know about the companies I recommended probably bailed out at the first declines. They also probably wound up hating me.

If you're enticed by some recommendations, I can't urge you enough to use my sound approach to check it out. It's only common sense to research the company, and study the numbers. Put the stock pick through as much rigorous examination as if it were your own idea.

Many times, people who recommend stocks offer very little to back up their views. That should be a warning to you. If someone can't support an argument, then there's a good chance there is no argument. You'll find unsupported stock suggestions more often on TV than in the newspapers and magazines; published accounts more often try to outline the reasons for selecting a stock.

I once witnessed firsthand the power of these TV stock evangelists. It was the autumn of 1994 when Snapple had taken a hard fall from grace. The stock was trading at about a quarter of its level in its heyday. I still thought it was a good company with excellent prospects. It seemed a good buy. I was confident the stock couldn't fall much further; at worst, it might remain stagnant for a while.

I happened to show up at Schwab one day and started chatting with one of the regulars. While we were staring at the Quotron, one of them asked me the famous question: "What stock do you like?" I told him I liked Snapple and rattled off my reasons. In effect, he told me I was crazy. He said that Snapple was a dead dog. His sole authority for his opinion, however, was some analyst he'd heard talking about Snapple on a TV show. He kept harping on the fact that this analyst thought the stock was lousy. He never mentioned why the analyst felt that way, if the wise one had even said. All that mattered was that this authority had made a sharply negative recommendation of the stock.

Finally I challenged the analyst's blind disciple: "What makes you think he knows any more than I do?"

Sure, that sounds cocky. But actually I was just confident.

All my life my parents have told me to be humble. They love that cliché that goes something like, "No matter what you do, there will always be somebody who can do it better." But when you really believe in yourself, confidence is all right.

I am very sure of myself when it comes to stocks. I'm convinced confidence is part of the winning attitude that every investor needs. What's more, if you believe in your own ability to pick the best stocks, you'll be less likely to fall for someone else's fishy recommendations.

You have to believe no one but you can make the best investment decisions. If you rely on yourself, you will keep your vision clear despite the blare of investment advice. That's not to say you shouldn't keep learning about stocks and studying the market. The more you learn, the more you'll have the confidence you need to make the right moves.

Just like Bobby Fischer. Even after he was the world chess champion, he continued to absorb everything about the game. He even listened to advice. But he didn't let it get in his way. I often think chess is a lot like investing in stocks. A good chess player keeps thinking several steps ahead. Both stock picking and moving chess pieces require careful deliberation and sound decisions. In both activities only you know what moves lie down the road. To get where you want to go you have to stick to your vision.

Imagine Bobby Fischer listening to some spectator sitting behind him in a chess match yelling out how he should move his pieces. If he'd allowed someone to dictate his moves, he'd never have been the champ. Similarly, you can't let a million voices tell you what stocks to pick. As soon as that happens, you not only stop believing you're the best investor in the world, you also severely limit your chances of ever becoming the best, or for that matter, even a good investor.

A Stacked Deck:
How Initial Public Offerings Bamboozle the Little Guy

It's hard not to get excited about initial public offerings, or IPOs. These are the often highly publicized first stock offerings companies make. The media love to play them up, highlighting the staggering leaps some of the new stocks make when they begin trading. Who can't recall one of the big names? Remember Netscape, the Internet-related software maker? It was priced at $28 a share and opened at $71, then closed on its first day at $58.25, more than a 100% gain. Boston Chicken didn't do bad, either. It shot up to $48.50 from an offering price of $20 on its first day. What about Snapple? It was offered at $20 and ended its first trading day at $29, a 45% gain. The list goes on: 3DO, up to $20.25 from $15. Barnes and Noble, up to $29.25 from $20.

What often gets left out of the discussion is that for every stunning debut, there is another stock that causes staggering disappointment. It may be a stock that began positively enough but then plummeted back to earth a short time later.

Or it may be a stock that sank like a stone from the get-go. People don't like to talk about that kind of thing.

The unflappable optimist may say, "Heck, I know some initial offerings don't work out but I'm willing to take my chances, given what happens when they do!" To him I'd say, "Not so fast!"

Besides the possibility of a tumble, initial offerings often send the small investor stumbling through a briar patch of obstacles that can leave him bloodied and bruised. As we'll see, the simple truth is that the deck is stacked against the little guy.

An IPO often makes good sense for a company. It provides an opportunity for the company to raise capital to fund future growth. Often IPOs are launched by relatively new companies that not only need cash but also want to gain some legitimacy by trading publicly. The IPO process requires a company to reveal its financial condition to the public. If the company is strong, the world will then know and the offering will likely succeed.

Companies tend to go public during bull markets. That's because in a rising market investors are always looking for new ideas, which often materialize in the form of hot newly listed stocks. A crummy company that doesn't even have a product can pull off a dazzling IPO in a booming market. If it has a cool name and good hype, the sky's the limit.

Bull markets also give rise to IPO fads. In the recent bull market, the IPOs of companies that profit from the Internet were welcomed with open wallets. One company called UUnet Technologies soared 86% in its first day of trading. The company makes software that allows computer users to browse the Internet. That IPO was followed by an offering from Spyglass, which produces similar software. Its price leaped 60% on the first day.

But try taking a promising company public in a down market. The poor mood among investors will doom the effort. When the market is suffering, new ideas are harder to sell—you probably couldn't even peddle the first shares of a company that just came up with a cure for cancer. You'll find that the number of companies attempting IPOs drops dramatically during poor market conditions.

The lure of catching the wave of a hot IPO is almost irresistible. Often everybody knows which stocks will skyrocket once they're listed. The hoopla is intense leading up to the first day of trading. An aura seems to surround the coming winners. You can feel it in the way people talk about the company. You can see it in the way the stock is hyped.

Sounds great, doesn't it? Seems like a sure bet. What an easy way to make a killing, you're probably thinking. Sure, some people get rich overnight on a brilliant IPO. But who are these people?

Ninety-nine percent of the time it isn't you and me. IPOs are arranged by investment banks working with the companies going public. They agree to buy the new shares and then sell them to the public—at a profit, of course. They're the underwriters. Depending on the complexity of the offering and size of the company, the investment bank may work with other firms to form a syndicate to unload the shares.

What all that means is that the investment bank and the firms working with them are interested in arranging big sales of the shares. They're not looking to sell you and me 300 shares at the initial offering price. They want to sell thousands and tens of thousands of shares, which doesn't leave much room for the little guy standing in the corner waving his arms and crying, "Hey! What about me?"

Of course, you can get in on the initial offering when the shares first start to trade. But you're not going to get anywhere near the best price, especially if the IPO is sizzling hot. In essence, what happens is that a hot IPO gets sold before it even begins trading. When the shares actually start changing hands, the price skyrockets. The Daddy Warbuckses who got in on the first floor ride the stock up several flights and then, satisfied with their one-day profit, unload it on you and hundreds of other poor Johnny-come-latelies at a price far above the initial offering price.

Now the question is: Will the stock continue to rise from its already inflated level? Sometimes it does. Other times it has reached its true value and hangs there stagnant. And worst of all, there are times when the run-up was unwarranted and the stock begins its return to earth just as you write your check for the purchase of the shares. In other words, you've sinned against all the morals I've tried to teach in this book: You've bought yourself a ridiculously overvalued stock.

It's not surprising that people get burned on IPOs, given the relative lack of information about the companies being offered. Since many of the companies are new and small, they often don't receive a lot of media attention until the IPO is announced. Then, as I said, it's difficult to separate the hype from the reality.

Trying to find information about these kinds of companies on InfoTrac or in *Value Line* and *Standard & Poor's* reports usually proves fruitless, too. You might be able to assess the company from the consumer's point of view. You'll have to track down where the company's products are sold, go there, and get a feel for how people are responding to them.

Given the limited information, you have to rely mostly on documents the company must by law submit if it wants to launch an IPO. The Securities and Exchange Commission requires companies to file a registration statement. This document gives a basic portrait of the company's business, its capitalization, purpose of the offering, expected price, estimated amount to be derived from the sale of shares, and other information.

Investors can get a summary of the information in the registration statement. Companies will send out these summaries, known as red herrings, so you can get an early peek at what's planned. The name red herring refers to a warning in red ink on the document that the information about the IPO may be incomplete. Investors will have to wait for the final prospectus—complete information on the offering—to be updated.

Despite all my skepticism about IPOs, I'm a little embarrassed to say that even I have given in to the mighty temptation they present. If it weren't for a stroke of good luck, I would have gotten burned royally.

I fixed my sights on a hot prospect, a direct marketer of personal computers called Gateway 2000. The company makes a line of IBM-compatible desktop, notebook, and sub-notebook PCs. I'd sized up the company and decided it was pretty good: It passed a lot of my tests. I'd also heard very good things about the company, partly because the hype was flying in all directions.

My cousin Philip was also excited about the IPO, and he encouraged me to pick up a few shares when they started trading. I rolled it over in my mind for days. Finally I decided to go for it.

My mistake was that I let my emotions get the better of me. I couldn't stop thinking about all the great IPOs of the past. I'd never gotten in on one of them. Now, it seemed, my chance had come.

The night before the actual trading day I phoned in my order: 400 shares. My dad wanted 600 shares; he, too, had given himself over to his emotions.

Luckily for me, I put a limit order on my request. A limit order simply tells your broker the price at which you're willing to buy the stock—you want it at either your stated price or better. I don't normally like putting a limit on my orders. It sets up the possibility of missing the chance to buy altogether. At the same time, a limit doesn't really fit with long-term investing. If you're going in for the long haul, you just want to get in. But it can be a godsend when you're wrestling with stocks short-term, as in the case of the risky world of IPOs.

I told my broker I wanted to buy the Gateway IPO at $15. If I couldn't get it at that price, forget it. The offering was priced at $12.

It was a school day so I set off for my classes, wondering what was happening to Gateway 2000 on Wall Street. At lunchtime, I raced to a pay phone to check in with my broker. I learned that the only price my dad and I could have gotten the stock at was $21.25 a share. So we missed it. My cousin Philip didn't get in either. But his friend picked up shares at $21 each. The stock closed at $22.

Not long after that Gateway 2000 plummeted to around $11 a share. It stayed there for a while, then managed to rally again. The last I looked it was up to $29.

Even though that's higher than I'd have gotten in, I'm glad I missed it. It would have been a tortuous road to that level, and who knows if I'd have had the stomach to hold on after the plunge to $11. I'm sure there are small investors out there still smarting from that one.

Reaping Your Profits:
How to Know
When to Sell a Stock

Is there any greater excitement than picking the right stock and watching it climb? You may think there's nothing better. But what about translating those paper gains into real dollars?

It's one thing to know when to buy a stock. As you've seen, a lot of careful thought goes into making a winning selection. Sure, it's a thrill beyond belief to see your stock bounce higher and higher.

However, it's quite another thing to know when to sell a stock. You can be the best stock picker in the world, but if you sell at the wrong time nobody is going to shower you with praise for your investment savvy.

Financial columnists like to scare people into thinking that knowing when to sell is the hardest part of investing. That's pure bull. They have a field day when the market drops. They start pontificating on the art of selling. They offer their smart ways to tackle a tough job. They suggest books devoted solely to selling stocks. Imagine a whole book on how to sell stocks!

It's lunacy.

Knowing when to sell is pretty simple. Though selling is a crucial part of investing, I still believe identifying and buying good stocks separates the amateurs from the pros. Knowing when to sell a stock is far easier than knowing which stock to buy. It's a treat to unload one of your picks after basking in its brilliant rise for a while.

If I ever get depressed about my investments, all I have to do is recall the time not long ago that I tasted the pure joy of selling a certain stock at a wonderful profit. It was that famous Chipcom, a maker of computer networking hardware, and it was my very best sale.

I bought the stock at about $34, and for a while it hovered around that price. Then it took a dive, sinking all the way to $22. But I'd identified it as a good stock, so I didn't panic. I didn't sell. I held on. Not only that, I was so positive about the prospects for this company that I picked up another bunch of shares at around the $22 level.

Over the next six months or so, Chipcom climbed. And climbed. It went to $50. It was then I decided the time had come to sell. I sold at $48 a share. My gain in that one stock was about 52%.

I bring up Chipcom because my experience with it exemplifies the rules I follow in selling stocks. First, it's important to point out that even though I insist on a long-term approach to investing, I can't emphasize enough that that doesn't mean investing forever. There will always come a time when you should sell.

Remember, even if you're a long-term investor, stocks are meant to be bought and sold. Be careful about falling in love with your stocks. If your attachment becomes too great, you will end up sitting by idly watching your stocks reach glorious heights and then sink down again.

The biggest mistake you can make is to form an emotional attachment to your stocks. It boggles my mind that some people develop such affection for their stocks that they feel bad about selling them.

A stock isn't your friend. It's a tool for making money.

So when do you sell? I keep a simple maxim in mind: What goes up must come down and what goes down must come up. That translates into what some people regard as a perverse way of looking at the notion of selling stock.

Simply put, I sell when a stock goes up too much. Because what goes up must come down. And I usually resist selling a stock when it slumps. Because what goes down must come up.

Recall my success with Chipcom. I finally sold that stock because it had climbed enough. Smart investors have a healthy fear of heights. Smart investors also limit their greed.

As your stock appreciates in value, you want to monitor various numbers to see how pricey it's getting. I can't really offer exact points at which to say the stock is so overvalued that it's time to sell. You just have to keep an eye on the price-to-earnings ratio, the growth to P/E measure and the cash flow per share level.

You really only know it's time to sell when your guts start to weaken and you begin to feel dizzy from the heights. A rule of thumb I use is that you don't want to sell until you've chalked up a gain of 25% to 30% on your stock. It's the only way to make good money.

Some people may balk at expecting such gains. They may fear losing a decent profit of, say, 10% to 15%, if they get greedy and wait for the 25% to 30%. After all, the stock could climb 20% and then slide way back before you sell.

Of course, that can happen. But I say again, if you truly picked a good company, there's a strong likelihood the stock will come back and even perhaps surpass the previous level. Even if it doesn't, you can wait for a return to the old level and this time you'll have a better feel for your stock and its price movements so you can feel confident about selling with the 20% gain.

If you want to sell at the right time, you have to keep a keen eye on politics, the economy, and individual industries. You may have a stock that's been doing great. Perhaps it's a defense industry stock that's gained substantially over the years and you're sitting on a pretty profit. Suppose then that a new president and Congress come into office vowing to reduce military spending.

The alarm bells should go off in your head. Cuts in defense spending, of course, will present a new and troubling environment for companies in the defense industry. Not only are future profits imperiled but an entire reorganization may be in the works. Indeed, that's pretty much what has happened.

And the impact on once strong defense stocks? They have had a dismal time.

If you're an alert investor, you'd pick up on that trend and sell your defense stock before the troubles actually hit, thereby securing your profit.

A similar scenario unfolded recently in the healthcare and drug industries. Amid much talk in Washington about changes in the healthcare system, those stocks went through some wrenching up-heavals. The savvy investor would have noticed the hints circulating in Washington through the media and dumped his healthcare and drug stocks long before the full impact was felt.

Politics can throw industries into turmoil. But it's also quite nat-ural for segments of the economy to undergo changes spurred by their own trends. Products can fall out of favor. Buying patterns shift. It takes a watchful eye to make sense of the many currents running through industries.

You must watch your companies for changes in the way they do business that fundamentally affect their operations. A company can take a new route that diminishes the strength you originally found so alluring.

Consider Rally's Hamburgers, which is a chain of drive-through hamburger restaurants. This was a high-flying stock based on the superior quality of the company's meat products. It was trading at a high of about $12 a share. But then the company started substituting a lower quality meat to boost its earnings. That move, along with other problems, took the wind out of its sails. The stock plunged to around $3.

The fundamental changes undertaken by Rally's Hamburgers would be a signal to sell the stock. But I learned the hard way that it's not always so easy to know when a stock really is dead or not.

Consider my catastrophic experience with IBM. What happened to me with IBM underscores the maxim that with good companies, what goes down must come up. I just lost my nerve along the way— a cardinal sin in investing.

My IBM debacle highlights the point that a decline in the stock's price should never be considered a reason to sell. I understood that when I was riding Chipcom's roller coaster. But I wasn't as smart with IBM.

The IBM story is well known. It was a fabulous company, a terrific stock in the 1980s. The stock was even considered a bellwether of the entire market: If IBM was breezing along so too would the rest of the market.

But in the 1990s the picture changed. The computer industry went through major shifts. IBM's mainframe computer business lost ground to the sizzling market for personal computers. Big Blue's earnings started to flag. The company began laying off workers.

All this couldn't help showing up in the stock price. From a high of around $150 a share, IBM slid to $100, then down to $55.

That's where I happened onto the scene. I saw IBM as still a great company, a real turnaround prospect. I was sure the stock had fallen far more than was justified. I applauded the changes under way: the firing of the former chairman and the hiring of Louis Gerstner, cutting of the dividend, the layoffs. The whole operation seemed to be improving its efficiency.

About this time, *Business Week* reported that IBM had a book value of $68. So I bought about 200 shares at $55, confident that I was getting a good deal. I figured all the bad news had already hit IBM, the numbers were soon going to look better, and of course, a rally in the stock price wasn't far off.

That's not exactly how it went. The stock hovered around $55 for a while. What happened next really kills me. The stock began sinking again, and it didn't stop until around $43.

If I'd been following my own advice at the time, I'd have held on. I'd have told myself that this was indeed a strong company with the potential to revive. Instead, I worried.

What's more, I magnified all the bad news I heard. My dad told me about an interview with some analyst on the radio who said there was a brain drain under way at IBM. That might mean all the talent that once made it great was abandoning ship. I listened emotionally, and I believed it all. I had lost my judgment.

If you remember the time IBM was declining and getting bashed in the press, you know it's hard to separate yourself from all that noise. It calls upon all your strength to stay the course.

But I didn't have it in me then: I bailed out. I sold all of my shares at $43.

IBM watchers know that soon afterward the stock climbed again. It didn't stop until it reached $100.

What I really kick myself for is that I knew what was supposed to happen. I'd thought it out. It went just as I anticipated; the stock climbed back up and the turnaround was successful. But I sold out because I lost my courage. I didn't follow my own advice and wound up making the worst investment of my career.

Missed Opportunity

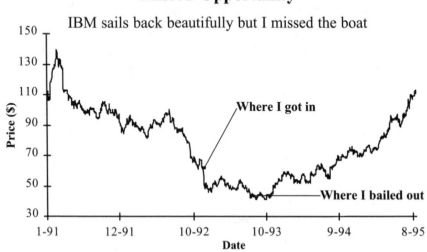

IBM sails back beautifully but I missed the boat

But the experience left me with a valuable lesson. It boils down to this: Never lose faith in yourself and your judgment. If you have done your homework and your stock pick meets your criteria, maintain your courage through the worst of times. You'll find yourself eventually arriving at the best of times.

In the IBM kind of circumstances you must remind yourself all the more that you *are* the greatest investor in the world. If you believe it, you won't falter. Make your decision with a clear mind and stick to your guns. What makes Warren Buffett so successful is that he doesn't waver once he makes his decision. He doesn't doubt himself, never thinks twice.

If you rely on your sharp skills and suppress your emotions, I guarantee you'll come up with far more moneymaking decisions than losing ones. Remember, if you've picked the right stocks, your chances of riding a lead balloon into the ground are limited. Instead, you're going to encounter a lot of IBMs that come bouncing back.

CHAPTER TWELVE

Building a Portfolio:
Forget Conventional Wisdom

Rewards Without Risk

There really are only two types of investors: those who have the time to be patient and those who don't. The design of your portfolio should partly reflect what type of investor you are. You should ask yourself how much time you intend to let your investments mature.

If you're twenty years old, you can take a more leisurely view of your investment horizon. You face less risk in general because you have more time to make up for any swings in the prices of your stocks. If you're middle-aged or beyond, you inherently face a higher degree of risk because you'll probably need to sell some of your stocks to cover expenses in your retirement sooner than a younger person. You could get caught having to sell at an unattractive time in the long-term price trend of your stock.

It's important here to clarify the meaning of risk. Many people confuse risk and volatility. They are two different things. As far as I'm concerned, risk in stocks is simply a measure of your time horizon. If you have a short time frame, your risk is higher because you may be forced to sell in a down market rather than ride it out and wait for the rebound.

Any way you look at it, the long-term investor wins. Since stocks appreciate over the long term, the investor with time on his hands can wait out any fluctuations and watch his stocks recover and even climb higher.

Risk is often misunderstood as these short-term price fluctuations. When investors worry about risk, they usually are concerned about their stocks sliding and washing them out. In fact, such short-term movement is mere volatility. Though important and scary, it's not much to worry about if you have chosen good companies and put your money on the line for the long haul.

Good companies will experience sharp, temporary swings in their stock prices. Sometimes it will be a move on the upside, sometimes it'll be a downswing. On the downside, people cry about the risk in the market. They worry about losing everything. The truth is that there is no serious risk if your company is truly strong and well run.

Nonetheless, everyone's first question when building a portfolio is, "How do I reduce my risk?" My answer is simple: Risk only comes from failing to do your homework and winding up with lousy companies. If you want to reduce your risk, follow the guidelines outlined in this book and buy good companies, then stay invested as long as you can.

Diversification: Excuse for Laziness

Take diversification, for instance. Stockbrokers and financial planners encourage diversification without even a flicker of doubt. They regard it as a rule of thumb for investing. Most of the time, their clients nod their heads and agree to the theory because it sounds so logical. Not only that, the investment adviser usually throws around the word diversification along with a lot of other complicated and sophisticated-sounding terms. For the investor, it's often easier to nod and agree than to stop the torrent of words and really find out what it all means.

If you take the time to think about diversification, you will probably realize—just as I did—that it's a fallacy. It fails to achieve its intended purpose. Unless, of course, the purpose is for your financial adviser to sell you as wide a variety of products as possible so he can collect as hefty a commission as possible.

Barron's *Dictionary of Finance and Investment Terms* defines diversification this way: "spreading of risk by putting assets in several categories of investments—stocks, bonds, money market instruments, and precious metals, for instance, or several industries, or a mutual fund, with its broad range of stocks in one portfolio."

I agree that diversification is a useful tool to minimize risk when you invest in a range of financial instruments such as bonds, precious metals, and stocks. You probably *should* worry about risk if you invest in bonds or precious metals. Often your investment in bonds is little more than a gamble on the direction of interest rates. And not even the Federal Reserve is able to predict the trend in interest rates. As for precious metals, everybody is aware of the unbelievable gamble you face with those investments. Most often, precious metals investments are based in some way on futures contracts, which are extremely risky and erratic investments only for the hardiest of souls. Purchasers of futures contracts buy or sell a specific amount of a commodity at a set price on a fixed future date.

For stocks, however, diversification isn't anywhere near as useful. Sure, people still think stocks are as much a gamble as anything, and diversifying your bets is believed the safest way to play. Many people's instincts tell them, "I don't really know what's going to happen and neither do you, so let's just cast a wide net and hope for the best."

That's a pitiful frame of mind with which to enter the stock market. What it tells me is that people who favor diversification are investors who lack confidence in their ability to pick stocks.

Amateurs aren't the only investors who lack confidence and hide behind the shield of diversification. Plenty of professionals suffer the same affliction. Diversification is an excuse for not spending enough time studying your stock picks. It's for those people who don't do their homework and pick stocks without fully evaluating them. The more effort you put into assessing each stock pick, the more confident you will be about it. And the less likely you'll need the crutch of diversification.

Don't think your local stock broker diversifies his own account only because he's a true believer in the concept of diversification. Just like the supposedly less experienced investor, he may have a natural insecurity about his stock picks despite whatever training he has. Even worse, he is probably insecure about the stocks he recommends to you, so he'll cover himself by telling you to diversify. He's scared out of his mind that he will give you bad advice and lose money for you. Then you'll dump him and find someone else to grab your commissions.

If your broker tells you to diversify and then your portfolio sinks, he has an easy out—he can blame it on the market since your diversification gave you greater exposure to the overall market. It ain't his fault.

Look at it logically. Doesn't it make a lot more sense to invest in a few companies that show definite superiority than to buy a whole bunch of companies you know only a little bit about? To my mind, it's a far safer strategy.

Warren Buffett describes diversification as the "Noah's Ark Approach." As he puts it, "You buy two of everything and you end up with a zoo instead of a portfolio."

Many proponents of diversification argue their point with the old saying, "Don't put all your eggs in one basket." Let's think about that for a second. How safe can it be to put, say, eight eggs in eight different baskets? All things being equal, you'd probably end up with eight weak baskets instead of one strong one. Not only that, it would be harder to keep an eye on all eight baskets. So your time would be diversified, too, and the care you give the eight eggs in separate baskets probably wouldn't equal the attention you could give to all eight in one basket.

I think it's probably wiser to put all your eggs in one basket.

I don't mean to suggest that you ought to invest your entire fortune in one stock. Only once in my life was my entire portfolio made up of one stock. It was Cybertek, and the reason I owned only that one company was that I couldn't afford any more stocks at the time. If four, or six, or ten companies are all top-quality, then by all means buy them all if you have the resources.

The point is: Don't diversify merely for the sake of diversifying. To counter those who blindly put forward diversification as the key to stock market success, I have my own rule of thumb: "Buy the best, forget the rest."

Slicing the Pie

Many proponents of diversification also like to throw around the phrase "asset allocation." It's simply the concept governing where in a broad sense you put the assets you have to invest.

The big brokerage companies have teams of people whose sole job is to crunch numbers and figure out the best portfolio mix of domestic and international stocks, bonds, cash, commodities such as gold and silver, collectibles such as art and antiques, and hard assets such as real estate. They come up with pie charts showing what percent of your assets should go into each category.

For most small investors, however, the pie would realistically have only three slices: stocks, bonds, and cash, if even that.

In December 1994, for example, some asset allocation gurus recommended that investors boost their exposure to overseas markets. They argued that the economic recovery that was then under way in the U.S. would spread to Europe and Japan, lifting their financial markets. William Wilby of the Oppenheimer Global Growth and Income Fund, for instance, recommended that investors put 41% of their assets in international stocks, 31% in both U.S. and overseas bonds, 16% in cash, and just 12% in domestic stocks.

Investors who followed this allocation guideline would have been disappointed, especially in the first half of 1995. The U.S. stock market sizzled in the first six months, with the Dow Jones Industrial Average gaining 19%. With just 12% of your assets in domestic stocks, your portfolio would not have gotten the full benefit of the rally.

A standard old formula found in Benjamin Graham's *The Intelligent Investor* promotes an asset allocation mix of 50% stocks and 50% bonds at all times. Some diehard 50-50 allocators believe that whenever one side advances the change should be offset by funneling the gains to the other side.

The formula would work something like this: Suppose you have $50 in stocks and $50 in bonds. If the stocks rise to $56 in value and bonds stay at $50, then you'd sell $3 worth of stocks and buy $3 worth of bonds. The transaction would readjust your allocation so that you would have $53 in stocks and $53 in bonds, regaining the 50-50 balance.

Graham points out that this 50-50 formula may be best for the conservative investor. The beauty of it is that it prevents investors from getting carried away by a rising market and pumping too much money into it, whether in stocks or bonds. That will limit the potential damage to one's portfolio when an inevitable shift in the rising trend occurs. On the negative side, of course, the investor won't reap rewards as stunning as other more venture-some players.

It makes sense in some cases to follow an asset allocation guideline. I mentioned before that some investments—such as commodities futures—are so volatile that it's wise to offset that volatility a little by including a few steady investments like certificates of deposit and some types of bonds.

Not only that, asset allocation helps investors ride out shifts in the economy. For instance, if you own a stock like Hayes Wheels International and the economy starts to weaken, Hayes may suffer because the auto industry will cut back on its orders of the company's products. At the same time, however, if you also have a good percentage of your assets in bonds, you will probably make up for the loss in Hayes. Bonds perform well in a weak economy because the great bugaboo to the bond market—inflation—is not usually a threat.

To take the possible benefits of asset allocation a step further, suppose inflation *is* a problem that's hurting both the stock and bond markets. If a piece of your allocation pie is in hard assets such as real estate and commodities, you will likely make up for the loss in the other parts of your portfolio. In an inflationary environment, many commodities including gold, silver, and oil often rise in price, as do property prices.

Beyond these advantages, asset allocation could prove worthwhile to those investors who simply don't have a long time frame. If you spread your investments over several categories, you're likely to minimize the volatility so that any sale of your assets will not be hurt by a temporary steep decline. By the same token, you may not reap the windfall of a steep rise, either.

For the investor with a short time frame, I'd recommend a portfolio asset allocation of the following type: 30% in domestic stocks (17% in value, 13% in growth), 15% in foreign stocks, 35% in short- to intermediate-term bonds (10% in foreign bonds, 25% in domestic short- to intermediate-term bonds) and 20% cash. The short-term investor who needs to be conservative also could use the 50-50 asset allocation mentioned earlier.

My asset allocation recommendation is aimed at constructing a hedged portfolio that will not decline precipitously in the down market. At the same time, however, it's unlikely to skyrocket along with a soaring market.

I opted for a larger amount of value stocks than growth stocks because typically value stocks move in a more consistent pattern with less volatility. Growth stocks, by contrast, are known for their erratic and extreme gyrations.

I've made short- to intermediate-term bonds a significant part of the portfolio because they pay off in a short time and aren't usually very volatile. Longer-term bonds tend to fluctuate, especially during periods of rising interest rates.

Foreign stocks and bonds are included as a way to hedge the portfolio even further. And the cash portion provides pure safety in just about any type of market.

Investors who do have a long-term outlook have less to gain from strict asset allocation. As I've shown, stocks over the long term outperform other assets. So if your time frame is lengthy, why mess with anything besides stocks? Forget bonds and commodities and real estate and art work. Build a portfolio that consists purely of stocks.

Of course there's one warning: If you can't find any good stocks, you would do well to look at other assets for investment. I, however, in my brief stock market career have never encountered a time when there weren't good stocks around. It could happen. There could be an awful economic cycle. Or the market could go up so much that it's impossible to find any decently valued stocks.

Remember my analogy about taking a rowboat across the ocean. If you can find only rowboat stocks, instead of stocks with aircraft carrier strength, I'd say it's safer to stay in port. You might make it across the ocean but it will be one heck of a journey.

Opening Your Wallet

Now that you have an idea of what to buy, it's a good time to discuss how to buy it and how much is reasonable to invest. You hear all kinds of bull about how much is a decent minimum to invest. I've heard some professionals claim that you have to have $400,000 to create a handsome portfolio that produces good returns.

No way!

Those people who toss around big numbers like that are the same ones who preach diversification—and they are the same ones who collect the fees on your investments. Is it any wonder they suggest big investments? The bigger the investment the bigger the commission.

I say if you want to buy a penny's worth of IBM, go right ahead if anyone will let you. The major concern, however, with very small investments is that the brokerage fees will eat you up. If I had to specify a minimum investment, I'd put it around $700. Once you invest less than that amount, unless your stock performs miraculously it's likely that you'll be at best treading water because of the brokerage fees.

You *can* do quite well with a small investment. Remember my first stock purchase. I put just $700 into Cybertek and three months later I was 114% richer.

Small but Steady Investments

Many people who don't have a large lump sum to stick into stocks follow a popular approach called dollar cost averaging. This strategy allows investors to put a set amount regularly into the stock market, such as a small portion of salary each month.

The advantage of a set dollar amount is that if the stock price is high you get fewer shares at the time of purchase. By the same token, if the price is low you get more shares at the time of purchase. The result is that your buying is occurring automatically pretty much as it should: You buy more shares when stocks are low and fewer when stocks are high. What you're doing, in essence, is blunting the impact of market swings on your portfolio.

I think dollar cost averaging is good in some respects. Since I firmly believe it's better to be in the market than not, you should come up with the funds to invest any way you can. It's far more effective to put money to work on a regular basis than wait and try to build up a lump sum, which in truth won't be that substantial anyway.

If you're lucky enough to have a decent-sized lump sum, the best move is to put it to work all at once. The worst decision would be to carve up that sum and use it for dollar cost averaging. If you have picked your stock carefully, you will be buying it at a good price that will likely rise because the company is strong. Again, you need the confidence to believe in your choice of stocks.

Studies have shown that when a stock rises you do better if you had purchased the investment with a lump sum rather than through dollar cost averaging. By the same token, however, when a stock declines you'll do better if you had bought the shares by dollar cost averaging rather than by forking out a lump sum.

The bold, self-assured investor (who is lucky enough to have some money to throw around) will always choose to take the plunge with both feet.

CHAPTER THIRTEEN

My Approach in Action:
Stories of Stock Picking

Best Buy

Lucky or Unlucky?

Best Buy is undoubtedly one of the best stocks I've ever owned. Investors in my mutual fund also have liked it a lot, considering the stock's great performance. The more you learn about the company, the more you like it.

Best Buy was a huge winner before I had a penny invested in it. It had already soared more than 1,100% from its low in 1990. I was just lucky to get in when I did. Or unlucky, depending on your perspective, since I got there so late. It is truly a terrific growth company.

Though it seems like an upstart company, Best Buy is actually thirty years old. It began life in Minnesota in 1966 as a retailer of audio systems called Sound of Music Inc. The name was changed to Best Buy in 1983, and it went public in 1985. The company started selling video equipment, microwave ovens, and major appliances in the early 1980s. In 1990, it inaugurated its current winning style, which is based on consumer-friendliness.

I first noticed the company when it started opening stores in the Detroit area. At the time, I happened to be checking out appliance stores because I was looking for a car stereo. I wasn't old enough to drive yet, but I believe in being prepared.

When Best Buy did roll into town it wasn't without some fanfare. Long before the stores opened, the company had a strong advertising blitz. You saw their ads in the newspapers and on TV. There were even flyers around touting the new stores.

It wasn't hard to see that the advertised prices had little trouble beating the competition. Not only that, the ads themselves caught my attention a lot more easily than the competition's. These were colorful newspaper pull-outs; for appliance store advertising, they were quite unconventional in their design.

I went in for my first look at the store two days after the grand opening and was thoroughly satisfied with everything I saw. Some things I had expected because I'd read about stores in the newspapers. But seeing it all in person convinced me that this company truly took a creative and innovative approach.

One thing I always like to point out is the store's policy regarding salesmen. You know what it was like before the Best Buy era. Most appliance stores used an unpleasant system that made pests out of salesmen. As soon as you'd enter, the guy would be there clobbering you with horror stories of what would happen if you didn't buy the more expensive appliance. And if you told him you were just browsing—well, if dirty looks could kill I'd be dead a hundred times already. Of course, under a commissioned salesman system you're only welcome if you're buying.

At Best Buy, it's a different world. There's no pressure. You're free to browse, take your time, make careful selections. Instead of the commissioned salesman, Best Buy has service centers—areas in the store where salaried employees welcome your questions. They can explain products well and they'll even point out the advantages and disadvantages of various products.

The Best Buy approach has several selling points. First and foremost, it makes the place consumer-friendly. If a store is known as a comfortable place to shop, people will come and sales will grow. Not only that, the approach improves the efficiency of the sales process overall by letting the customer decide what he or she wants and then buy it. Instead of badgering customers, store employees are free to do other tasks. But they're there when they're needed. Overall, with fewer salesmen, the company's costs are lower.

The store is consumer-friendly in another important way. What consumer, myself included, doesn't love fiddling with the devices on display? At Best Buy, you're not only allowed to fiddle, you're encouraged to do so. Imagine this: You're in a store packed with fabulous gadgets and the salesmen are relaxed, or nonexistent. The gadgets are just waiting for your fingers to crawl all over them. Well, go right ahead!

That's what sets Best Buy apart. At other appliance stores, you have a salesman who wants to demonstrate everything for you himself. That's a bore and doesn't let you interact with your potential purchase. You could take the thing home and not know anything about it. Or you have a salesman who shoots dirty looks at you when you test how high the volume goes on that high-powered stereo.

At Best Buy, there's a Speaker Theater where you're actually *supposed* to test the range of the products. There's also an area where you can play a variety of video games.

Contrary to popular belief, kids aren't the only ones who like to play around with all the appliances. I've seen plenty of older people checking out a lot of details including every little feature of the video cameras.

The user-friendly and comfortable atmosphere is deceptive, however. If you take a closer look, you realize the stores are really dressed-up warehouses. It's to the stores' credit that they use warehouses and can make them look so pleasing. After all, the warehouse setting further shows that the operation is low-cost and efficient. Best Buy can provide comfort and variety more cheaply than its competitors.

All this efficiency translates not only into fatter profits but also better prices for consumers. Best Buy makes sure everyone knows that its prices are the lowest around. If the competition tries to undercut prices, you can be sure Best Buy will offer a lower price. If you can find the same product somewhere else at a lower price after buying it at Best Buy, the company will refund the difference. That's not a one-time special—it's the company's policy.

Best Buy has had a major impact on pricing in the industry, especially in music compact discs. Before Best Buy rattled the competition, you were lucky to get a CD for $18. That was the price practically everywhere. At Best Buy, you pay $10 to $11 for a CD. Other stores have responded by lowering their prices but not to the level of Best Buy's.

Connecting with the Customer

The salesman policy and the store design are clearly great, but the real question is: How do customers respond to the company? You can have the most user-friendly store in the world but if no one walks the aisles and plays with the gadgets, the store will be a bust.

No worries on that score with Best Buy. The consumer reaction to the new stores was nothing short of breathtaking. This enthusiasm among the customers had a profound effect on my opinion of the stock.

I wasn't immune to the excitement. I constantly begged my mom to take me to the store. Going to Best Buy was close to a fad— and not just among kids my age. At parties I heard the older kids talking about the place. Adults also got into the game. I used to listen while my parents and my forty-year-old cousins eagerly discussed their own visits to the store. They talked about it in a tone of voice I'd heard used for Heather Locklear or Christie Brinkley. That clearly said something to me. After all, it wasn't some gorgeous woman they were all worked up about—it was an *appliance store*.

The same conversations must have been going on in other houses, too. If you looked at the checkout lines at Best Buy you realized that people were pouring out of their houses and filling up their shopping carts. Every cash register was open and brimming with bucks.

I also realized that this wasn't a phenomenon just at our local store. Best Buy was expanding throughout our area and meeting with equal success everywhere. The fact that the company was popping up all over the place further brightened my outlook for the stock. A company's expansion isn't necessarily a reason by itself to buy the stock, but it *is* a positive signal about the company's health. Best Buy was expanding not only in the city of Detroit and the suburbs but also fairly aggressively throughout the country.

As I began to notice Best Buy, I started thinking about the state of the appliance store industry. Usually I don't study industries very closely because I'm a bottom-up investor who analyzes the strengths and weaknesses of individual companies. But in the case of Best Buy, as I got very interested in the stock, I delved into the industry to better understand the company.

In the days before Best Buy, the appliance store industry was dominated by several dinosaurs like ABC Warehouse, Fretter, and Highland Appliance. It's not that these stores were awful, it's just that they weren't very good. The whole appliance store industry seemed rather boring with no great stocks to offer.

Stores sprang up now and then to compete with the old dinosaurs but created little stir. They were often mom-and-pop shops or regional chains. But they all looked the same to me. The new ones looked just as drab as the old. They all had cheaply lighted interiors with salesmen in cheap suits. Neon lights outside promised unbelievable deals. And if you dared to go inside, the salesmen would insist the owner was ready to cut you the deal of the century; it was only for you because you had the wisdom to come to his store!

Best Buy was light years away from all that. When I noticed how different the company was, it really had me jumping. I began to come up with comparisons for the impact Best Buy would make. It's not usually the wisest idea to compare something unknown like Best Buy to companies that have already become legends, but I couldn't help myself from thinking that perhaps what I'd discovered was another Toys "Я" Us or Dunkin' Donuts.

Let me give you an idea of how great this stock was before I bought it. A look at the company's numbers back in 1990 reveals the potential of Best Buy stock. I'm going to walk you through some of those numbers so that you can see in concrete terms what a fabulous stock looks like in the early stages. After all, the whole point here is to find tremendous stocks while they're still just small fry.

I should be satisfied that I had a good run with Best Buy. But still I can't help kicking myself again because I didn't have the opportunity to see the stores back in the early 1990s when the company instituted its new design and sales concept.

Consider this. In early 1991, Best Buy was trading at $1.80. Let's say you were on to this company and sank $10,000 into its stock. Now fast-forward a few years. Rightfully, you're a little cocky. You might even think yourself a genius. You recognized a winner. You took the plunge, sat back and watched the number of stores expand and the profits grow.

Now, in late 1994, you decide to sell your $10,000 stake. You don't want to be too greedy. There always comes a time to take your profits. And what profits they are! The stock has climbed from $1.80 to $40. Your $10,000 has turned into about $220,000, not counting brokerage fees.

Now let's look at how you might have read the company's numbers back in 1991 and sniffed a winner. In 1991, you'd have had to use an annual report detailing 1990 data; so the numbers we'll use here are for 1990.

Our first area of inquiry is the debt-to-equity level. The figure is *not* terribly exciting. Debt totals 53.1% of the company's equity. That's rather high. Remember, a standard level would be a-round 25%.

Next, you study the return on equity. Here again, you're not bowled over by the 9% level. I would have liked the return on equity to be at least 25% for a company like Best Buy.

To be fair, however, you recognize that the company is expanding swiftly at this time. So these numbers may not be beautiful but they are understandable. In 1989, Best Buy operated forty-nine stores. In 1991, it had seventy-three, an increase of 49%. Those less than wonderful debt and return-on-equity numbers are part of the cost of expansion.

On the more positive side, you notice that the company's net income in 1990 totals $5.68 million with a cash flow of $11.2 million. The cash flow works out to 1.97 times net income, which is pretty

Solid Company, Solid Gains

Best Buy, my best pick, adheres to the law of "What goes up must come down, and what goes down must come up"

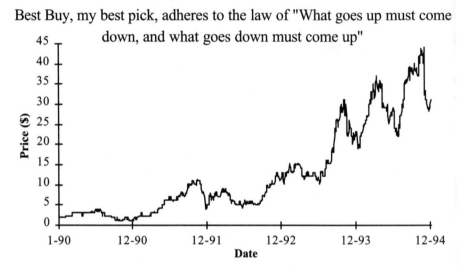

good. To me, it's a very good sign when cash flow equals two times net income.

It is also encouraging that the company's profit grew 17.8% during the year, while sales expanded 14.8%. I also like the fact that the company wasn't paying any dividends; instead, the money that might have been doled out to shareholders as dividends was plowed back into the company to boost earnings.

What adds to the attractiveness is that at $1.80 a share, you're getting good value for your money. This is measured by the price-to-earnings ratio, which is 10. Not only that, the company's growth relative to its price-to-earnings ratio is positive at 1.7.

A further look at the company's value offers still more reason to be interested. The cash flow to price sends a clear signal that you're getting a lot of strength in the company for a decent price. The figure is .2777; in other words, the stock's price is 3.6 times the cash flow (the reciprocal of .2777). If the standard is for the price to be about 10 times the cash flow, then this level of 3.6 times suggests that the company offered quite a good value relative to other stocks.

Good Bang for Your Buck

Now let's look at the book value. In 1990, Best Buy had a book value of $2.28 per share. Considering the stock was selling at $1.80 a share, that book value of $2.28 per share is impressive. Though I sometimes criticize the way book value is calculated, I still have tremendous respect for what it tells you about a company. With the share price so much below the book value, you can be pretty sure you're getting a good bang for your buck out of this stock. The comparison of book value to share price indicates that the stock is cheap.

If you put all the aspects of this stock together—everything from your impressions about its operations and its numbers—you can't help but conclude that Best Buy fits the profile of a winning stock. Even though a few numbers aren't as strong as you might like, all told, the stock is superattractive.

At least that was the picture in 1991. The stock performed as might have been expected. In one year, Best Buy climbed from $1.80 to $11.80 for a gain of 655%. And the rally wasn't over.

You would have been quite lucky to recognize the potential of Best Buy in 1991. It's truly rare for anyone to get into a stock at the very best moment and get out at just the right time. But that doesn't mean you can't make a nifty profit by coming in a little late. That's what I did with Best Buy.

Let's fast-forward to late 1993, when I actually bought the stock. The previous discussion about Best Buy in 1991 was the dream scenario. Now as I show you how I got into the stock in 1993, we return to the realm of reality.

As we know, the company looked great if you walked the store aisles and studied the way it was managed. Many people would have been persuaded by those criteria alone to purchase the stock. But as I've tried to emphasize, you have to look at the numbers, too. Otherwise, you're taking a blind leap of faith.

In September 1993, Best Buy was trading at about $17 a share, adjusted for stock splits. For the most part, the usual numbers I assess appeared about average and in some cases above average.

One definite improvement was in the debt-to-equity ratio, now at 9%. That was a steep decline from the 53.1% in 1990 and far below the standard of 25%. It was also encouraging that the company's inventories were declining after rising for the last few years.

Cash flow also looked very good. It was more than double net income.

On the downside, the company's return on equity was a dismal

8.2%. Ideally, I'd want return on equity at around 25% or higher. I was also a little worried that the company may have been expanding too fast. The number of stores had soared: in 1989, there were 49; in 1991, 73; in 1992, 111; and in 1993, 151.

Other numbers were pretty good: earnings growth at 35%, cash growth at 29%, and sales growth at 46%.

The next question to consider was the stock's price level. I wasn't thrilled. At the current level, the stock was trading at a price-to-earnings ratio of about 25. That was far above the P/E of 10 in 1990. But the growth-to-P/E ratio looked attractive at 1.4. In fact, that number was among the best in the heap.

Further analysis of the stock's price level revealed nothing terribly exciting. The book value was $5.29 per share, so at $17 the stock was selling quite far above book value. In other words, at the current price you were paying about three times the level of the company's assets. Cash flow per share was $1.01, which is slightly below the 10-to-1 standard.

The argument in favor of buying the stock at this time isn't nearly as persuasive as it was in 1991. You don't have the stock selling below book value, nor do you have the low price relative to the company's earnings.

But this scenario does provide a good lesson in how much your own judgment comes into play in picking stocks. What do you do when the numbers aren't hollering at you to buy the stock but at the same time aren't screaming out a warning to run away?

The answer goes back to what I said about the need for flexibility in the process of stock selection. Just as the big automakers learned there wasn't only one way to build a car on an assembly line, so there isn't only one scenario for choosing a stock. The stock investing world isn't so smooth that your decisions will be clear-cut. Far from it. You have to balance one thing against another and weigh both of those against a third, and so on.

That's partly what makes the process exciting. No two situations are the same. Remember the three simple guidelines: You must gather and draw on your knowledge about the stock, think independently, and assess the situation logically.

Let me show you how I confronted the question of whether to purchase Best Buy in 1993, given the less than clear signals I got from the numbers. In the first place, I was very excited by the company based on my observations of the stores. With that in mind, I already was willing to give up a little on the numbers. My reasoning came down to two main points: 1) The company was extremely attractive from a non-number point of view; 2) Though the numbers themselves may not have been stellar, they certainly didn't raise any red flags.

Logic told me the stock was a buy.

What all this shows is that even I don't follow my own process rigidly. I'm always ready to see things for what they are and am ready to adjust my thinking. Of course, the process would have been much easier if the numbers had all pointed in one direction. But since I was willing to take a long-term view, I felt confident about the ultimate strength of Best Buy. Even if it had plunged right after I bought it, I would have held on knowing I'd found a solid company. I might even have sold other holdings to buy more of the stock at the lower price.

Fortunately, I didn't have to consider such options right away. The stock rallied shortly after I bought it, climbing from $17 to its all-time high of $31.40 in about three months.

Then the stock hit some rough waters. It began to sink, and sink, and sink. If I had followed my own advice, I probably would have sold the stock long before the decline began. I'd have taken my profits on the way up and gotten out.

But I held on. I'm not ashamed of my decision. I think that the reason I kept the stock was simply my outlook for the company. No matter what went on with the stock, I believed Best Buy ran an excellent operation. From the very start, my outlook was long-term and didn't waver from it. When you have a long-term view, you shouldn't be swayed by short-term price swings.

Too Much, Too Fast

Nonetheless, I have to say that when the stock tumbled to $19 from its high of $31.40, I was momentarily disheartened. Who doesn't want their stocks to climb endlessly? But I wasn't seriously concerned since I saw nothing in the company's operations that threatened to tarnish Best Buy's position as a solid company and great stock. The price had risen too much, too fast, and was going through an adjustment.

In fact, earnings were growing nicely. In 1992, the company earned 57 cents a share; in 1993, earnings expanded to $1.01 a share. At $19, the stock price was far more attractive than it was earlier. The price-to-earnings ratio had slid to 16 from 25.

I concluded that the stock slid largely because the price had soared too much too fast. It was time for an adjustment. Not only that, probably there had been another weird random move within the market. I took comfort in one of my laws of the stock market: "What goes up must come down, and what goes down must come up."

Lo and behold, the law proved true! After hovering around $19 for a little while, Best Buy resumed its upward move. This time, it climbed to $36. I'd learned my lesson and decided to reel in some profits. So I sold my shares at about $33 each. I was very happy with my experience.

But my interest in Best Buy wasn't over. I still regarded it as a good stock and planned to watch its price very closely, waiting for a nice decline to provide another chance to buy.

An opportunity eventually arose as Best Buy ran into some heated competition from the giant in the appliance store business, Circuit City. Circuit City has been around a lot longer than Best Buy. It began operating in 1949 in Richmond, Virginia, as a one-store retailer of TVs and other appliances. The company went public in 1961. In 1975, it pioneered the electronics superstore concept with a $2 million gamble in Richmond.

The bet paid off. Circuit City went on to become the nation's largest consumer electronics chain, with two to three times as many stores as Best Buy.

The company would have seemed a formidable rival to Best Buy. But, in reality, the two stores didn't clash head-to-head until very late in the game. For one thing, Circuit City pretty much targeted the east and west coasts, while Best Buy concentrated on the Midwest. Not only that, Best Buy couldn't really be considered a serious contender to Circuit City until the 1990s because it was still a tiny David to Circuit City's Goliath.

But when the two finally did move into each other's territories, the competition heated up. I would have been foolish not to take a close look at Circuit City, primarily as a competitor and then as a potential stock pick. After all, Circuit City had been a dazzling stock for many years. From 1973 to 1983, it had soared 4,713%. From 1983 to 1993, it was up another 1,124%. Now consider this: If you'd bought the stock in 1973 and held it for twenty years, you would have racked up a spectacular gain of almost 60,000%.

So why didn't I think Circuit City would overtake Best Buy? It's a great, well-run operation, but still it represented the old style in the appliance store industry. The company still used armies of salesmen to push products on every customer who walked in the door. It's my sense that the company prided itself on its salesmanship.

I did a close comparison of the operations of Circuit City and Best Buy and, frankly, came up with a stalemate. If you look at the cost structure of each company, Best Buy comes out ahead with the lowest costs in the business. Its overhead-to-sales ratio is 15.3%, compared with Circuit City's 22.8%.

But Circuit City has a stronger profit margin of 3.2%, compared with Best Buy's 1.2%. Circuit City also has little debt because it relied on internal resources to finance its expansion. Best Buy's debt level is rather high.

You could easily say that the two companies are pretty equal. So how do you break the stalemate?

For me, the final piece of the puzzle is the consumer angle. If everything else balances out, you have to ask yourself which store the consumer would ultimately prefer. As I said, Circuit City has great stores in a traditional style. The company doesn't do anything terribly new; it just does the old things better than anybody else.

Best Buy, on the other hand, represents the future. Its stores and its style are fresh and innovative. I'd always banked on Best Buy continuing to grow and prosper. If there ever came a battle to the death with Circuit City, I'd put my money on Best Buy.

So when the stock sank after I sold my first batch of shares I was eager to buy again. By July 1994, Best Buy had sunk to $22 from $37. The $22 level turned out to be the bottom. I started to buy shares again at $29 and continued buying through some subsequent price declines, so my average price worked out to about $23 a share.

The stock then climbed to a new high of $45 a share over the next six months. I happily took my profits at around $41 a share.

Chipcom

Another Michael Jordan Stock

If my portfolio were a basketball team, Best Buy would be Michael Jordan. In order to win, you need to give Michael Jordan the ball a lot of the time. For my portfolio to win, I need to pump money into my best performers like Best Buy.

I've been fortunate to have another stock perform for me with as much razzle-dazzle as Michael Jordan. And that's Chipcom.

Remember 1994? It was a pretty lousy year for stock investors. That was the year the average mutual fund lost 2%. Most major market indexes also declined, while the Dow Jones Industrial Average struggled to a 2% gain.

By contrast, Chipcom vaulted higher and higher in 1994. I put a lot of my money in it, and as a result by year's end I was basking in a 70% gain from this one stock, which did wonders for my fund.

In some respects, the decision to buy Chipcom marked something of a departure from my usual style of investing. As you well know by now, I take a long-term perspective on a stock. I want to buy companies that thoroughly demonstrate they have strong prospects for the long haul. I like to observe the companies firsthand. I want to walk the aisles of the stores, or use the products.

Best Buy was clearly a consumer-oriented company with a great long-term outlook. The company seemed destined to become a legend and eventually to dominate its industry. Best of all, I could visit its stores and see for myself whether they were properly run and thriving. The stock price had already had a good run. But I wasn't concerned because the strong price just reflected the market's vote of approval.

Chipcom was quite another story. The company did demonstrate some characteristics of a solid long-term bet. But that wasn't my primary interest in this case. I liked Chipcom because it was an undervalued growth stock. Despite my tendency to hold stocks for a while, I had an early feeling with Chipcom that I'd get rid of it rather soon after buying it.

Rewards of Reading

I became aware of Chipcom in an unusual way. Chipcom's business is rather arcane: It involves providing the ability for computers to hook up with one another and communicate. Chipcom's products help companies set up efficient and successful computer networks. I couldn't go down to the mall as with Best Buy and see what the company does.

In fact, I'd probably never have known about the company if I hadn't been flipping through *PC Week* one day and seen an article that got me thinking. So I did some more research: I studied the computer networking industry. I read a lot and talked with my cousin who's a computer consultant. Before this time, I had no idea what type of networking systems companies needed.

Gradually, it dawned on me that Chipcom's products were a key to pushing the industry forward. I knew that networking was already well advanced. Nonetheless, there was always room for improvement, and Chipcom seemed to be poised to grow fantastically.

The company was incorporated in 1983 and entered the networking market in 1985. It went public in 1991. The company sells what is called intelligent switching systems that allow different per-

Patience Is a Virtue

Holding on to Chipcom proves successful

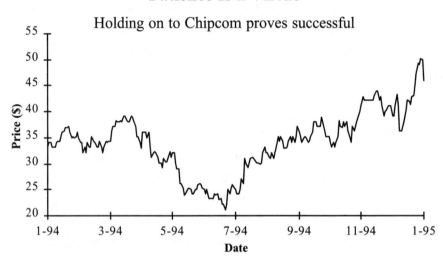

sonal computers to communicate with each other, even if they use different languages.

The company's products were highly regarded and got strong ratings in computer magazines. Chipcom was said to be in a very strong position in the industry, with products that were far above the competition.

But still I didn't fully understand what was so great about the company. Remember, you should never buy a stock if you don't understand what the company does. It wasn't until I had it explained simply to me by a friend who'd studied the company carefully that I appreciated the superiority of Chipcom. It also didn't hurt to learn that Chipcom sells about a third of its products to IBM and that it had teamed up with Big Blue in 1992 to work on networking products.

A Better Link

In the simplest terms, my friend explained that Chipcom's products helped improve the way information is passed among computers hooked up on a network. In earlier days, a network would have Computer A, Computer B, Computer C all the way to, say, Computer K. If Computer A wanted to communicate with Computer K, it would have to pass information all the way through the network from its own Computer to Computer B, then on to Computer C, and so on until the information got to Computer K. If there was a problem with, say, Computer D, the information wouldn't go through.

Chipcom eliminated the problem. Its technology allowed Computer A to communicate directly with Computer K, bypassing the other computers in the network. My friend added that at the time no other company was able to do this so successfully.

All that was left for me to say was: "Wow."

That was one hell of a company.

Having determined that the company looked great from a distance, I decided to move in for a close examination: It was time to see if Chipcom's numbers met my requirements.

I was pleasantly surprised. In fact, the numbers were truly the reason I bought the stock. Look at the Chipcom balance sheet on page 155 to see what I mean.

First, as usual, I scanned the company's debt-to-equity ratio. It was an attractive 0.01. But you expect a low debt level in this kind of technology stock because these companies don't require a lot of capital for production, unlike an auto manufacturer, for instance. Other companies in the same industry had little or no debt, such as 3Com with a debt-to-equity ratio of 0.05, Cabletron with no debt, and Cisco Systems also with no long-term debt.

While low debt levels are good, it only takes you so far. Another key number for Chipcom was its profit margin. Common sense tells you that if the profit margin is increasing and inventories are decreasing, future earnings are probably going to be bright. Between 1989 and 1993, Chipcom's profit margin was quite positive, climbing from 5.8% to 9.5%.

Other numbers, taken together, added up to inspire confidence in the stock. Chipcom's return on equity was 12% over the previous twelve months. It was even higher, an acceptable 15%, over the last five years. Cash flow to net income was somewhat less than great, but at 1.51 it ranked well above average among its competitors in the industry. Cisco, for instance, had a cash flow to net income of 1.08, while Cabletron was at 1.25.

Chipcom Corporation

CONSOLIDATED BALANCE SHEET

(in thousands, except per share data)

	December 31, 1994	December 25, 1993
Assets		
Current assets:		
Cash and cash equivalents	$ 10,698	$ 10,857
Short-term investments	41,322	58,239
Accounts receivable, net of allowance for doubtful accounts of $3,801 in 1994 and $1,613 in 1993	45,319	27,789
Inventories	58,701	25,864
Prepaid expenses and other current assets ..	4,830	2,153
Deferred income taxes	11,351	5,144
Total current assets	172,221	130,046
Fixed assets, net	34,495	17,925
Intangible and other assets, net	15,137	9,957
	$221,853	$157,928
Liabilities and Stockholders' Equity		
Current liabilities:		
Current portion of long-term debt and notes payable	800	$ 4,010
Accounts payable	25,627	11,964
Accrued expenses	22,955	12,931
Income taxes payable	3,559	437
Total current liabilities	52,941	29,342
Deferred maintenance revenue	4,843	2,355
Long-term debt	**284**	**1,058**
Deferred income taxes	4,849	480
Total liabilities	62,917	33,235
Commitments		
Stockholders' equity:		
Common stock, $.02 par value: Shares outstanding—16,775 in 1994 and 15,866 in 1993	124,847	108,958
Retained earnings	34,089	15,735
Total stockholders' equity	**158,936**	**$124,693**
	221,853	$157,928

Reprinted by permission of Chipcom Corporation. (Chipcom merged with 3Com Corporation of Santa Monica, California, in October 1995.)

Low debt, high prospects: Chipcom's balance sheet reveals a solid company with the opportunity to grow. Note that long-term debt is less than 1 percent of total stockholders' equity. That tells you the company's liabilities won't hamper further expansion.

Astounding Growth

Offsetting these numbers was Chipcom's astounding profit growth. Remember that I said one absolute requirement of a stock is that it have a positive growth rate. Well, Chipcom more than met that requirement. Chipcom's earnings per share were growing at a blistering 88%. Total sales were up 75%. And net income was soaring at a growth rate of 116%.

But what about the stock's price? The numbers that measure price weren't spectacular. With such phenomenal earnings you wouldn't expect a terribly low price-to-earnings ratio. Chipcom's P/E was fairly high at 37. Cash flow per share was $2.06, and book value was $12.07 per share. Both weren't great but they weren't worrying. The growth to P/E was the most attractive of the price ratios, coming in very strongly at more than two.

Even though the numbers didn't scream out that Chipcom was a fabulous value, if you looked at the price in terms of the company's potential you had to say to yourself there was still good value in the stock.

All things considered, I decided to buy Chipcom at $36 a share, but I didn't buy much. I was still dedicating my resources to stocks like Best Buy. That didn't leave much money for new additions to the portfolio. Still, I liked the company a lot and I thought it was a heck of a stock.

Soon after I got in, the stock raced up to $40. But then Chipcom plummeted. Right after it hit $40 a share it began to fall and it didn't stop until it hit a low for the year at $21.

How I kept my nerves intact amid such a plunge is still a wonder to me. But I did hold on. It's impossible not to feel edgy and ready to bail out at times like that. But fortunately I didn't panic. It would have been a serious mistake.

I tried to keep clear-sighted and look at the stock realistically. In the end, I decided the stock was falling for no concrete reason. The tumble was caused mainly by a few Wall Street analysts who had downgraded their investment view of the stock, mostly because it had climbed so high. When a stock shoots up, analysts sometimes lose their enthusiasm for it simply because it is more expensive. But the outlook for Chipcom and its market still looked very bright. Indeed, the company's prospects were still pretty much the same as when I examined the stock at the $36 price range. Sure, the growth rate had slowed a little but it was nothing significant or unexpected.

The result of the stock's sharp decline was that Chipcom was now a bargain. Its price-to-earnings ratio had fallen to 24. The P/E might even have fallen lower if the stock price had remained stagnant and the company reported earnings at the low end of expectations. Some scenarios called for a P/E as low as 17, which would make the stock extremely cheap. Under that scenario, Chipcom's earnings growth rate could have dropped to 48%. It could have slid even lower and the stock still would have been very attractive.

Consider this. A growth rate of 48% may not look great next to Chipcom's earlier numbers. But that level of profit growth is still terrific. Of course, you have to consider why growth is slowing, even at that level. And the only reason I found was that it was due to seasonal factors. I concluded that the correction in the stock price was drastically overdone.

It seemed to me that Chipcom was poised to prove once again the truth of my basic stock market law: What goes up must come down, and what comes down must go up. Before I'd made my initial purchase Chipcom had had a sizzling run—up more than 85%. It was impossible to ignore the healthy prospects for the company and its industry. Even if net income didn't grow at more than 100%, as it had been, so what? Fast growth was still in the cards.

So I decided to take advantage of the bargain-basement price. I unloaded my shares in Schwab and sold some shares of a few other holdings and bought as much as I could of Chipcom. I didn't buy it only for myself but grabbed as many shares as I could for my dad's IRA, too. Our price was $23 a share.

I was prompted into action by two considerations. First, I reasoned that the stock couldn't fall very much further, given that nothing fundamental had changed and that the company remained strong. Second, I believed that the upside potential for the stock was tremendous. It was not only that there were no clear signs of any fundamental changes, but also that Chipcom's market was far from saturated and its products were superior.

After all, I thought the company was a good buy at $36. So why wouldn't I think it was a fabulous buy at $23?

Well, as you might expect, the story has a happy ending. Chipcom proved to be one of my most profitable investments. It helped me stand out in the investment world as most of the Wall Street pros were licking their wounds.

Soon after I made my second purchase of Chipcom shares, the company reported higher earnings and analysts began upgrading their views on the stock.

The rally was a beauty to behold. Chipcom climbed from the $23 level to a high of about $51, adjusted for splits. I sold my own shares and my father's at about $48 each for a total profit of more than $35,000.

Blockbuster Entertainment

An Ideal Stock

Few stocks illustrate the beauty of my investment approach better than Blockbuster Entertainment. If you used my stock-picking process to evaluate this company, you would have easily identified a prime prospect. In many ways, Blockbuster is an ideal stock.

I kick myself for missing this one. Regretfully, I never invested in Blockbuster or for that matter even considered it as an investment. It just slipped by my radarscope.

That happens. But it's not the end of the world. Besides, there's a lot to learn from studying the ones you miss.

Anyone with a VCR probably knows that Blockbuster is a chain of video rental superstores. It didn't begin life in that form, however. David Cook launched the company in Dallas in 1982 as Cook Data Services, and took it public the same year. It sold software and computing services to the oil and gas industries. But as the energy industry slowed in the mid-1980s, the company shifted direction. In 1985, it opened its first video rental store. The name was changed to Blockbuster Entertainment the following year.

The company became an astounding success partly because of its timing. It caught the early wave of the video rental business and ran wildly with it. The stores were the first of their kind in the industry. No other video rental outlets had the flashy presentation and enormous size of Blockbuster stores.

Blockbuster opened its first store in my area about a mile from my house in Troy. Before its arrival you could almost feel the demand growing for video rental stores. Sales of VCRs were booming—as far as I could tell practically everybody had one. It seemed to me the primary function of a VCR was to play rented videos, since buying the movies was so expensive.

In Troy, as across America in the mid-1980s, the video rental game was in its early stages. There were two stores in our town. Both were mom-and-pop operations with a limited number of titles. Some grocery stores, record shops, and convenience outlets also had little video rental sections.

And that was about it.

All these places did fairly well simply because of the growing demand and the limited number of rental locations. If an industry is growing, the small outlets can do well; they don't have to offer a spectacular selection or be terribly efficient. They just have to be pretty good at what they do.

But when a company like Blockbuster comes along, watch out. Clearly, its executives saw the potential market. And Blockbuster had the capital to move in. It's expensive for a mom-and-pop shop to carry many copies of a box office hit. Distributors typically charge more than $70 per tape for the megahits.

Not only that, if you want to meet the strong demand for video rentals you need a huge number of titles—and that requires a quality computer system to manage the inventory and generally run the store. That technology is expensive. The mom-and-pop operation would ordinarily cringe in the face of these costs.

Blockbuster's sheer size made it almost invincible. How could any small store compete when it typically carried only 3,000 titles compared with Blockbuster's 10,000? With so many titles to choose from, customers would be inclined at least to come in and browse at Blockbuster.

When I'm out with my friends, we sometimes stroll into Blockbuster just to look around. The design of the place makes it exciting and fun to be there. And no one seems to care if you want to browse the collection for a while. In fact, Blockbuster makes you *want* to be there.

That's part of what underlies its success. As with any retailing operation, the key is to get the customer in the store. Once the buyer is there, the chance of a sale (or rental) is of course vastly improved. My friends and I often leave with a tape even though we had no idea what we wanted when we walked in.

Blockbuster's size paid off in another way. Traditionally, video stores' business is hit-driven just like the movie industry. If you carry the big movies, you don't need to bother with the lesser titles. Because it's so huge, Blockbuster is able to carry not only the hits but also older or little-known movies. These are cheaper for the company to purchase yet they rent at the same price, so the break-even point is lower. That adds up to higher profits.

Some service innovations also paved the way for success. At Blockbuster, you can rent tapes for three evenings whereas other shops let them out for only twenty-four hours. The policy encourages customers to rent more than one tape at a time.

Shunning X-rated movies, Blockbuster instead loads up on children's titles. The place is inviting to families; it's fun for kids to join their parents on rental outings. TVs often play kids' movies to occupy the young ones while mom and dad search for a title. Not surprisingly, a extra few bucks winds up being spent on a kids' tape or two.

Unlike the mom-and-pop operations, Blockbuster lets you pick the actual tape and bring it to the counter yourself. This gives the customer the sense of having more control over the selection and rental process. It's also more efficient. At other shops, a customer finds an empty box on the shelf, takes it to the counter, and waits while the employee digs up the tape—if it's available.

Good Hours

Blockbuster's hours ensure a good flow of traffic. As a chain, the company can get employees to work shifts to keep the outlets open from ten A.M. to midnight, seven days a week. If mom and pop tried to compete with those hours they'd be dead from exhaustion in no time.

So it isn't surprising that Blockbuster killed the competition. Within a couple of years, the other video rental shops in our area were out of business. You could still get videos at grocery stores but they weren't any threat to the giant.

From Blockbuster's point of view, a fabulous thing had happened. Even if we wanted to rent videos elsewhere, we really didn't have any other decent options. We were forced to go to Blockbuster. That certainly doesn't hurt business.

Walk in there at eleven at night and you won't be lonely. The superstores are doing business practically all the time. Often they don't seem crowded, but I think that's an illusion created by the boxy design and huge size. There are more people in there than you might suspect.

A positive sign for the company and its stock was its expansion. In the late 1980s, Blockbuster expanded at a blistering pace. There were 133 stores in 1987; by the end of 1988, the number was 375.

Overall, Blockbuster would have passed the first part of my process with flying colors. From a purely subjective and observational point of view, it looked like a fantastic prospect. In this way, it was a lot like Best Buy. The two companies created excitement in their industries; they were innovative, well run, and efficient.

The second part of the process—an examination of the company's numbers—also would have jangled the bells in favor of Blockbuster. In fact, the true superiority of this company really emerges in the numbers.

Let's look at the way the company stacked up in 1988, the year I wish I'd noticed it. At that time, Blockbuster's debt-to-equity ratio stood at 21%, which is very attractive in general terms. And when you consider the company was expanding so rapidly at the time, a ratio that strong is literally eye-popping.

The cash-flow-to-net-income ratio also checked out very favorably. It stood at about 2.6, which measures nicely against the ideal level of 2 or above. Return on equity was at a very decent 15%.

What was really astounding was the company's growth. Not just earnings but revenue, cash flow, and book value. All these areas were expanding at a rate of about 100%.

Given Blockbuster's fast growth, you'd expect the stock price to be so high it was untouchable. Not so. The P/E was an undaunting 25. The growth-to-P/E ratio was 4, quite attractive when you consider that 2 means the stock is quite cheap. Other numbers were all right and not discouraging for a small company at the time that was growing very fast.

The stock price at the evaluation point in 1988 was $3, adjusted for stock splits. From there, it climbed to a high of $34 in 1993. The stock then retreated a bit. In September 1994, Blockbuster was purchased by Viacom. At the time, the stock was trading at $28 a share. As far as I can tell, Viacom got itself a great property at a great price. No doubt the shareholders ended up happy. I would have been, too.

CHAPTER FOURTEEN

Mutual Funds:
An Easy
Alternative to Stocks

If the Shoe Fits . . .

Nobody believes more than I do in the benefits of investing in individual companies. It's educational, thrilling, and profitable. But it's also hard work.

For many reasons, individual stock picking is not for everyone. You need look no further than the booming mutual fund industry for proof. Indeed, mutual funds are perfect for some people.

Consider my dad. He's always had some money he needed to invest, either for his retirement or to help pay college expenses for three children. But he had no interest in financial matters. In fact, the whole idea of money repulsed him. He knew he needed to think about investing wisely but he didn't want to waste his time managing his money.

Every year he'd just hand over a check to his stockbroker to invest in his Individual Retirement Account. He rarely checked on the state of his portfolio. He assumed everything was okay and his investments were growing.

Surprise, surprise!

One day he and my mom took a serious look at the records only to discover that his account had actually lost money. He'd been so unconcerned about his investments that instead of building a little nest egg he'd been crimping his future.

Someone like him—who needs to invest but wants to keep his distance from the process—is the perfect customer for a mutual fund. In fact, he was one of the reasons I decided to set up my mutual fund. I realized that my dad and sisters and cousins all fit the profile of the typical mutual fund investor: a person who has neither the time nor the enthusiasm for individual stock research. I had a feeling I could help them to do better with their investments than their stock brokers. Not only that, they wouldn't have to get their hands dirty with the investment process. All that was left up to me—their personal money manager.

To be honest, there was another motivation for me to start my fund. Call it the Big Dream. At that time, when I was fourteen, I didn't have a lot of money of my own to invest. I needed cash to make cash. If I could pool my family's money then I'd have a little bundle to work with. My goal, of course, was to get rich. And I intended to do it the way the greatest investors—Peter Lynch and Warren Buffett—did it: by pumping the money into stocks.

I had every intention of building the Matt Seto Fund into the size of Fidelity's Magellan Fund, the nation's largest mutual fund with more than $50 billion under management at last look.

For the record, my mutual fund isn't a mutual fund in the truest sense. It's a limited partnership. The two are fairly similar in that they both pool money and have an expert managing the money for others. In a mutual fund, the investors are shareholders. In a limited partnership, they are limited partners in the fund.

I chose to go the route of a limited partnership for several reasons. First, it's much cheaper and less complicated to form a limited partnership than it is to launch a mutual fund, which requires wading through mountains of paperwork and paying thousands of dollars. For all your trouble, you have to abide by the many rules governing the operation of mutual funds and you're also closely watched by the Securities and Exchange Commission.

A limited partnership, by contrast, costs only a few hundred dollars to form and merely requires the eye of a good lawyer. Not only that, it is a less regulated investment vehicle. So you have more freedom in moving from one type of investment to another; in fact, you can invest pretty much any way you want.

Investors in my fund do face some hurdles. For one thing, no one except family and close friends are allowed to invest—that's the law laid down by my dad. And for those lucky or unlucky enough to get in, I make some demands that other investors would likely resist. For instance, I require my family and close friends to invest for the long term. I make it difficult for them to put their money in and get it out quickly. Also, some investors might balk at my unwillingness to diversify. Then there's always a lot of joking about my qualifications as a money manager. While my family does consider me an investment expert, I don't exactly fit the profile of a "professional."

Giant Universe

Investors in standard mutual funds have a staggering array of choices. The industry has undergone such explosive growth that there are now more mutual funds than there are stocks listed on the New York Stock Exchange. In 1974, investors could choose from just 431 mutual funds; now there are more than 4,600, according to the Investment Company Institute, compared with about 2,700 stocks listed on the NYSE.

In a broad sense, there are two types of mutual funds: open-end and closed-end. Most mutual funds are open-end; that means that the number of shares in the fund expands to accommodate demand among investors. A closed-end mutual fund, by contrast, has a set number of shares. Unlike an open-end fund, the closed-end variety trades on an exchange just as a common stock does. In this chapter, I discuss only open-end mutual funds.

Clearly, interest in mutual funds has grown because of their many advantages. You can buy and sell a standard mutual fund just as easily as a stock and you get a whole lot more than just one stock. Indeed, one of the chief attractions to many investors is the diversification you get with mutual funds. With their huge sums of money (usually at least $10 million), mutual funds can buy a lot of different stocks.

This is particularly beneficial to the small investor who would never be able to own such an array of companies on his or her own. Even though I'm not a big fan of diversification, I can see the advantages for some investors to spread their money out among the many companies in a mutual fund. It is particularly useful for those people who, in essence, invest blindly—they may know a little about the mutual fund and next to nothing about the specific companies it holds. In a large sense, their investment is a gamble but they lower their risk because the mutual fund contains many stocks.

A Professional at the Wheel

One of the primary attractions of mutual funds is that you get a professional to manage your money. You can feel a little more comfortable knowing the person making your investment decisions is probably well educated, fully trained, and at least somewhat experienced.

The same could be said of a stockbroker, but if anyone's going to guide my investments I'd prefer it to be a mutual fund manager. Don't get me wrong—there are a lot of good, trustworthy stockbrokers who come up with fine stock picks and make money for their clients. No matter how you look at it, if you do need help you're better off to have any professional direct your investments—whether it's a stockbroker or mutual fund professional.

I favor mutual fund managers because they are rewarded for their performance (which is also your performance), and wouldn't you want someone whose interests are directly tied to yours? A stockbroker, by contrast, doesn't make money from the performance of your portfolio; he gets rich from the number of transactions he performs for you.

The usual advantage of a broker is that you get personal service. But if your broker is good, he'll likely be popular, which means he'll have less time to spend with you—especially if your account isn't huge. And many stockbrokers set clients up with a portfolio of mutual funds. So why not invest in the funds directly yourself and save the commissions? Anybody—anywhere—can invest with the best mutual fund managers by simply picking up the phone.

Sheer convenience is one of the top selling points for mutual funds. Like my dad, many people simply don't like researching individual companies or have no interest in it. For that kind of investor, nothing ever created was more convenient than a mutual fund. These investments put everything into one package: diversification, professionalism, and ease of purchase.

But wait. Before you forget everything you've read in previous chapters about stock picking on your own, consider the downsides of mutual funds.

First, the performance of mutual funds isn't that great. Sure, there are periods when some funds perform spectacularly, and sometimes even a broad range of funds will do quite well. But overall, the performance of the entire group falls short. According to the book *A Random Walk Down Wall Street* by Burton G. Malkiel, 66% of mutual fund managers failed to beat the market during the past two decades.

Who's to say individual investors relying on their own smarts can't do better than that? In fact, maybe there's a fallacy in the belief that a professional manager is going to deliver better returns than the amateur. I'd say that those investors who are willing to devote a little time to research and follow this book's guidelines will wind up with better results than those professionals.

There is no way to measure how individual investors have performed over the years, but perhaps you can get a glimpse by looking at how investment clubs have done. The National Association of Investors Corporation, which works to educate the individual investor and serves as an umbrella group for investment clubs, says that 44.5% of its chapters have performed as well as or better than the S&P 500 stock index for the life of those chapters.

It isn't entirely clear why mutual funds underperform. But I suspect one reason is that they are forced to abide by certain rules that impair the maneuvering of their managers. One obstacle is the rule imposed by the Securities and Exchange Commission that prohibits a fund from investing more than 5% of its total assets in one stock. For instance, if I run a mutual fund with $200,000 in assets, I can't own more than $10,000 of any one stock.

Another rule states that a mutual fund can't own more than 10% of any one company. Together, the two rules tie the hands of many fund managers. Suppose a stock is soaring but the fund already has 5% of its assets in it. The manager can't buy any more shares and his performance will suffer for that. Likewise, suppose a fund already has a 10% stake in a certain company and the company's stock takes off. The fund will benefit from the rise but not as much as it would if it could boost its investment.

Now imagine that a fund is invested up to its limits in the great companies but it has a pile more money to invest. In order not to keep that money on the sidelines, the manager must put it somewhere. So he may be forced to invest in inferior-quality stocks, weighing down the performance of his fund.

Checking Out the Menu

Despite their drawbacks you may still find that mutual funds suit you. You may not want to put all of your assets in them. Some people use mutual funds for part of their portfolio and make up the rest with a selection of individual stocks. In any case, if you do decide to explore mutual funds, you'll find you have a big menu of choices. Most people agree that stock mutual funds break down into five broad categories:

- Equity income
- Value
- Growth
- Sector
- Specialty

Equity income funds normally invest in stocks that pay high dividends. The goal is to provide most of the investor's return through dividends and to limit the volatility of the fund.

Value funds invest in stocks the manager believes are undervalued. The goal is to provide income and capital gains with relatively little volatility. These funds are somewhat similar to equity income funds.

Growth funds invest in companies with better than average earnings prospects. The aim is to provide strong capital gains but the risk is high volatility.

Sector funds may not appeal to the average mutual fund investor. That's because they don't provide the usual broad diversification associated with mutual funds. Instead, these funds take a narrowly focused investment strategy. They invest in many stocks, but practically all the investments are in one industry such as technology, retailing, financial services, or health. If you're in a hot industry, the rewards can be fabulous; but if you're not, it can be painful. In other words, these funds tend to swing in wide fluctuations.

Specialty funds are also sometimes classified as sector funds because they include sharply focused portfolios that might concentrate on a certain industry or on small companies or Asian-Pacific stocks. But specialty funds may venture into areas far beyond the realm of a sector fund.

Making Your Selection

Before you can begin to consider specific mutual funds you must define your objectives. Do you want fast but risky growth? Or are you the type who wants steady, safer appreciation? Your answer will help determine the type of fund you need.

For instance, a retired person who doesn't know when he or she will have to draw on the money in the mutual fund account will probably prefer a less volatile investment. In that way, if there is an emergency and the money is needed, there isn't so much risk that there will be less money available because of some steep downward fluctuation in the fund's performance.

By contrast, a young couple also investing for their retirement may prefer an aggressive growth fund because of its potential for large gains. The young couple are less worried than an older person about temporary sharp declines because they know they won't draw on the money in the fund for many years. They have the time to ride out the fund's likely volatility.

Once you know your objectives you can move on to analyzing the funds themselves. It's a lot trickier to single out a good mutual fund than it is to find a good stock. You have to make qualitative judgments. There aren't any reliable hard numbers to point you in the right direction. You can't look at the statistics on debt to equity or the book value because these numbers don't exist for a mutual fund.

Remember, whenever you compare funds make sure you compare funds of the same type. You don't want to compare a growth fund to an equity income fund. Likewise, you want to make similar time frame comparisons. If you're looking at one fund's performance over three years, look at your comparison fund's results over the same period.

Many people often believe that all you have to do is look at the fund's performance to know whether or not it's a good fund. If that's your sole criterion, you're taking a big risk. Just look at what the mutual funds say in their own advertising. T. Rowe Price, for instance, cautions: "Past performance cannot guarantee future results. Investment return and principal value will vary and shares may be worth more or less at redemption than at original purchase."

Peter Lynch has a way of summing up the debate over whether past performance is any indication of the future. His Peter Principle is: "You can't see the future through a rearview mirror."

Critics might offer a strong rebuttal: "History repeats itself."

But if you look at the mountains of studies investigating the question, I'm afraid you can't help but conclude that the Peter Principle wins. The studies show that mutual funds that have performed well in the past don't necessarily perform well in the future—just as T. Rowe Price admits.

Some of the biggest names in mutual funds aren't shy about telling it the way it is. John C. Bogle, chairman of the Vanguard

Group, tackled the issue in his book, *Bogle on Mutual Funds: New Perspectives for the Intelligent Investor*. His conclusion: "Avoid funds at the top of the performance deck with hot recent records. Particularly avoid funds that are bragging about it or whose managers are lionized in the press. Hot funds never fail to cool off."

Bogle suggests that if you do analyze performance, the longer the time frame the better. A fund that's hot for one year isn't nearly as attractive as one that's been climbing consistently for a decade.

The simple fact is that you can't avoid at least looking at the past performance. Right or wrong, our evaluations of most things— whom we hire, whom we promote—rest on past performance. Our views of presidents, congressmen, and basketball players all are based on what these people have done so far in their careers. Likewise with mutual fund managers—we should look at their careers and the history of their funds.

Nuts and Bolts Analysis

Though there are no sure answers, you can improve your chances of a good mutual fund selection by assessing the fund's manager and fees.

When you look at a fund's performance you get a view of its manager. How a fund does rests solely on the manager. Performance is a measure of his ability to pick good stocks and buy and sell them at the right times.

Analyzing the manager of a mutual fund is a lot like examining the management of a company. In both cases, you try to evaluate the effectiveness of people you don't know and probably can't get to know very well. Most of the time our opinions are based on secondhand information, either from the media or the company's own promotional material.

So how do you figure out if he or she is a good fund manager or not? Unreliable as it seems, we come back to the question of performance. (You can see why I like to invest in individual companies: You have so much more to work with when appraising your investment.)

Nonetheless, you can benefit by looking at a few aspects of the fund manager and his performance. Carefully study the fund's performance in recent years. Even though many studies warn against making too much of the fund's latest returns, it's a simple fact that you have to look at performance. If it's a hot fund, find out if the manager has been with the fund for as long as it has performed well. Sometimes, for whatever reasons, funds change managers. So a performance record may apply to the fund but not the manager. If the manager has been working at another fund, find out his performance there. Again, this approach doesn't add up to a sure bet but it's the best you can do in trying to make a sound decision.

For another angle, consider the perspective of Peter Bernstein in his book, *Capital Ideas.* Bernstein writes, "Recent research demonstrates that some mutual fund managers may have 'hot hands' and others may have 'icy hands.' A fund that performs well one year is likely to perform well the following year, and the same is true of a fund that performs poorly."

Of course, hot hands can turn cold for any number of reasons. For instance, a hot fund may attract a huge inflow of money. But all that cash can create problems for the fund manager. He may be unable to find enough decent investment opportunities for it all and wind up buying companies that don't perform well.

The best advice is to satisfy yourself about the fund's investment style—does it meet your objectives?—the reputation of the mutual fund company, *and* the historical skill of the portfolio manager himself.

Fees are also a top consideration. There are two basic fee structures for mutual funds: either no-load or load. A no-load mutual fund doesn't charge you to buy shares. A load fund, by contrast, does have a fee. Supposedly, you get some advice from the person selling you a load fund, whereas no advice is available when you buy a no-load fund. You can face other costs such as management and redemption fees, so always find out up front what you'll be paying to get into any fund.

Fees can run up to 2% of the amount you are investing, and sometimes more. That means you have to do all that much better in the fund to come out with a decent gain. If your fund gains 10%, you wind up with an 8% gain after fees. The bottom line is that you want to keep your fees as low as possible.

Since the early 1990s, some brokerage firms have started making it cheaper to buy mutual funds. Charles Schwab, and later Fidelity, set up programs that eliminated transaction fees for many mutual funds.

As for me, I don't charge a transaction fee on my fund, either. Originally, I had big plans to rake in money from my investors. In my prospectus, I warned that I'd take 15% of any gains over 6%. That plan was modeled after Warren Buffett's early partnership in which he took 25% of any gains over 6%. However, I dropped that strategy. It seemed a little unfair to cream off some of the profits from my own family and friends. Besides, I always felt they were doing me a favor by investing as opposed to my doing them a favor by managing their money.

Doing Your Research

Just as with individual companies, you want to find out as much as you can about a fund before you invest. There are two main resources for mutual fund information: *Morningstar* and *Value Line Mutual Fund Survey*.

These two services are to mutual funds what *Standard & Poor's* reports and the regular *Value Line* surveys are to individual stocks. While stock investors need to supplement the information in these kinds of sources, the mutual fund investor can get just about everything he needs right here. It's not that the mutual fund services are any more comprehensive than the individual stock reports. Rather, it's that since mutual funds are set up to be as convenient as possible, investors simply need to know less.

With these two services, you have at your fingertips everything you need to be a good mutual fund investor.

Morningstar very comprehensive. You find information about the fund's objectives, its style, and its investments. There's a capsule biography of the manager revealing where he went to college, his degrees, and his previous experience. A graph traces the performance of the fund through the years and shows any changes in the investment style.

The *Morningstar* report also provides an analysis of the fund's risk. You can eyeball the fund's twenty-five biggest holdings, its weightings in different sectors, its investments in stocks that make up the major indexes, its holdings of foreign stocks and small- and mid-capitalization stocks. The report includes information on the size of the companies the fund has in its portfolio. You can determine if the fund holds any other types of investments such as options or futures. A breakdown of the fees also is featured.

One easy-to-use aspect of the report is the star ratings. *Morningstar* measures the fund's returns against its risks and comes up with a rating. Funds with the highest returns and lowest risk are awarded the most stars. The best rating is five stars.

The *Value Line Mutual Fund Survey* provides about the same information, though it seems to me a little less comprehensive. It's a matter of personal preference.

Wading Through the Prospectus

Besides using these services, it's a good idea to pick up a copy of the mutual fund's prospectus. It contains some useful information about the managers and the fund's history and objectives as well as other data. In essence, it tells you what to expect and what not to expect. As a rule, the prospectus warns investors that they should read the thing thoroughly before they write any checks.

But frankly, if you pore over *Morningstar* or *Value Line* you're just as likely to know what you're getting into. Not only that, you'll probably have an easier time understanding everything. A prospectus isn't always the most clear and comprehensive document you'll ever read. In fact, a lot of it is deliberately vague and general. Sometimes it's downright confusing. These documents are often written by lawyers in their native tongue.

I'm as guilty as anyone. I know I didn't go out of my way to make it easy to read the prospectus for the Matt Seto Fund. Many people who read it told me the most interesting part was the drawing on the cover. I did the drawing myself. It shows me flexing my muscles, hoisting my dog in my right hand and a dollar bill in my left.

Some investors may want to peruse the the mutual fund's annual report. It resembles a company's annual report except that it's far less glitzy. It contains a letter to the shareholders that sometimes has some useful tidbits, a statement of liabilities and assets, and a listing of all the fund's investments and the amount of each owned.

The media also churns out information on mutual funds at a dizzying pace. With the booming growth of the mutual fund industry, newspapers and magazines are stumbling all over each other to attract fund investors as readers. Entire magazines, such as *Mutual*

Fund, are devoted to information on—what else?—mutual funds.

Frankly, I find all this information for mutual fund investors a little silly. As we've seen, you can't get that much information that's truly of any use in assessing prospects for a mutual fund. The performance numbers, which most of the media harp on, are only partly useful in analyzing funds.

What's more, I wonder why mutual fund investors would even read most of what's printed. Mutual funds are supposed to be an easy and convenient way to invest for people who don't want to take the time to study too much. So why would mutual fund investors want to keep so abreast of every quiver in the market and the industry?

I'd argue that all the information only makes mutual fund investors more jittery than they should be. It probably encourages them to buy and sell more than they should, too.

If mutual fund investors truly are so interested in the financial world that they are spending hours of time reading about mutual funds, then they would be far wiser to invest in individual stocks. They should use the time to research companies, study their numbers, and find strong long-term prospects.

CHAPTER FIFTEEN

Roads to Success:
Identifying Winning Situations

In Pursuit of Happiness

With stock investing, our goal is to find the happiness that a rising stock brings. How we pursue that goal depends on our own personalities and tastes. Some people simply have an inclination for one style of investing over another. I, for instance, would be strictly classified as a growth stock investor, someone who seeks out companies with consistently strong growth. I most enjoy finding good growth stocks for investment, while someone like Benjamin Graham is categorized as a value investor, someone who prefers stocks that are selling at a price below their real value. Two other standard situations that attract investors are cyclical stocks and turnaround stocks. In this chapter, we'll look at the four winning situations—growth, value, cyclical, and turnarounds—to see what makes each one work.

Though the roads to success break down neatly into their four distinct categories, there is some important overlap that you should be aware of. While I would generally call myself a growth stock investor, it would be more precise to say I'm a growth investor who looks for value. What makes me happy is to find a growth stock whose price doesn't reflect its true value. In other words, I like growth stocks that are cheap. I'm constantly on the lookout for situations that combine the two categories of growth and value.

And there lies the key: finding stocks that are a good value. Though value investing is considered a discipline of its own, I have found that in all four of the winning situations, you're really just looking for different ways to capture value. For instance, if you prefer cyclical investing you want to identify as best you can when a stock has fallen to the low point in its cycle, presenting you with the best value. In turnaround investing, you want to buy a stock when the company's fortunes have hit bottom and are poised for a rebound. At that time, you're likely to get the best value for your dollar.

Crossing Disciplines

Some investors have been able to master more than one winning situation, though I don't think it's necessary for making money in the stock market. I stick pretty much with my value-growth discipline. That's not to say I don't think a lot about the other situations.

Crossing disciplines can be profitable. Benjamin Graham, who is probably more identified with value investing than anybody, racked up big gains in the insurance company GEICO Corporation, a growth stock.

As far as I know, the only person who could invest successfully in just about every area was Peter Lynch. That ability is what sets him apart from mere mortals—it defines his genius and lies at the root of why he did so phenomenally well in the market. In some respects, he was forced to be a great investor across disciplines because his mutual fund, Fidelity Magellan, was so large. With billions of dollars to invest, he had to find every possible nook and cranny that looked good. Inevitably, the search took him through the various situations of growth, value, cyclical, and turnarounds. While he succeeded with a huge mutual fund because of his versatility, other money managers have faltered when their mutual funds grew too much; these less versatile players aren't able to navigate along the different roads to success as well as Peter Lynch.

Becoming a highly versatile investor is far less important for you, unless you plan to manage the Magellan fund some time soon. What you need to do is find the situation that makes you most comfortable. And remember that no matter what situation you prefer, you can use the process outlined in this book to determine the quality of your potential stock picks. Though I emphasize growth stock investing, my process can help alert you to danger signs and prevent unhappy mistakes.

INVESTING IN GROWTH STOCKS

Since this book has been occupied with describing the methods—and rewards—of growth stock investing, I don't need to say much more here. But I'd like to add a few important points.

Growth stocks are companies whose earnings climb consistently. It doesn't matter if the economy is faltering—these companies, often providing essentials such as food and medicine, will continue to report solid profits. Lately, technology stocks have become the darlings of growth stock investors while some of the old standbys such as the drug makers have fallen from favor. The earnings of growth stock companies not only rise in a consistent manner, they also usually notch up bigger gains than other companies.

Growth stock investing is the standard way good long-term investors build their fortunes. Coca-Cola has long been considered a popular growth stock. Need I reiterate its rewards to the long-term investor? If you'd bought a mere one share for $40 in 1919, you'd be sitting on 47,904 shares and $3.2 million today. Indeed, most big companies today from U.S. Steel to RCA to Xerox were once considered growth stocks.

Since growth stocks are long-term investments, you want to analyze them with a long-term horizon. Your perspective is slightly different than it would be for, say, a cyclical stock where you're likely to hold it through the next cycle, then try to sell it at the top. With growth stocks, as we've seen in this book, you buy and hold.

INVESTING IN VALUE STOCKS

Value investing boils down to figuring out what you're getting in a company for the price you're paying. As with anything, a good value is something of quality purchased at an inexpensive price. The same way you want to weigh a product against its price tag, you want to compare a company and its operations to the level of its stock price.

Though I emphasize that I seek out growth stocks with an eye to their value, I have to say that in a pure sense there's a big difference in the way you analyze the two types of stocks, growth and value. If you were looking at just growth or just value, you'd take two distinct approaches. Since I often combine the two disciplines, I have combined the two approaches in my process. Remember that I said buying stocks is a two-step process. First you have to identify a potential company. Then you have to evaluate it carefully. The first step relates to the growth stock aspect, while the second concerns the value side.

In essence, my process combines two opposite approaches. In growth stock picking, you rely on many subjective considerations.

You try to assess the intangibles about a company. That's why I always want to visit a store like Best Buy. I want to get a feeling for the company. In value investing, however, decisions rest solely on the numbers. A strict value investor sees how a company's numbers stack up and then either buys or passes on a stock. At the risk of repeating myself (but I will because it's such an important point), I stress that it makes supreme common sense to back up your instincts with numbers and back up your numbers with your instincts.

Nonetheless, many investors do rely just on the numbers and largely ignore subjective analysis. These value investors ponder such numbers as the debt-to-equity ratio, the return on equity, the P/E ratio, the price to book, price to cash. Some toss out the company's historical growth rate numbers, believing that the past doesn't say anything concrete about a company's future. More reliable, they say, are figures relating to debt since they give a genuine picture of the stock's risk.

Price, Price, Price

The most important aspect for the value investor is the stock's price. Just as with any purchase, you weigh the product against its price tag. If you don't like the price, there's practically nothing that's going to get you to buy the thing. That's why value investors look so closely at numbers that relate directly to the stock's price, such as the P/E and the price to book. What has to be determined is whether the stock is priced below what the company is really worth. No true value investor will buy a stock unless this criterion is met. In that investor's eyes, the stock doesn't have the potential to rise unless it's below the company's true value. The belief among value investors is that stocks will eventually rise to match the level of the company's true value.

A stock can be cheap, and still not be priced below the true worth of a company. A strict value investor wouldn't be interested in a cheap stock. But *I* could be, because I look at the intangibles in addition to the numbers. If I see a stock that looks enticing for subjective reasons and it's cheap though not trading below the company's worth, I may very well buy it. That's because I may recognize a strong growth possibility in the company. I may see the potential for the stock price to far exceed the company's current value. So, in the strictest sense, I wouldn't be buying a value stock but rather a well-priced growth stock.

If you do plan to follow a strict value investing approach, it's important to realize that you're probably not getting in for the long haul. Value investors must have a pretty well-defined target at which to get out. Since these investors buy in anticipation of a stock's price rising to its appropriate value, they should be prepared to sell when that value is reached.

Suppose, for instance, you bought Cosmos stock at $40 a share. Let's say you used book value as a way to determine the true worth of the company. Your calculations put book value at $60 a share. So when the stock approached $60, you'd be getting close to full value. For planning purposes, you'd probably set your sell target at around that $60 level.

INVESTING IN CYCLICAL STOCKS

Cyclical stocks tend to rise and fall with the ups and downs of the economy. If the economy is strong, then the earnings of these companies grow; rising earnings are the route to rising stock prices. Similarly, if the economy weakens, so do earnings of the cyclicals; weak earnings wreak havoc on a stock price. Cyclical companies include those in housing, automobiles, chemicals, and paper.

Successful cyclical investors keep a close watch on the big picture of the economy. They need to have a good understanding of economic trends. You don't need to be a Nobel Laureate in economics, but it's certainly useful to have a keen appreciation for the many influences working within the economy. The aim is always to know how your investments stand relative to the economic outlook. Failure to recognize a shift in the wind could prove painful for your portfolio.

The cyclical investor also has to watch what's going on in various industries. Though cyclical stocks do tend to move in a fairly predictable fashion, they don't all move at the same time for the same duration. Certain industries such as autos and apparel makers usually rise first when the economy begins to pick up. They're followed by later-stage cyclicals such as steel and chemicals as the economic momentum improves.

If you're tempted to become a cyclical investor, you had better first ask yourself one crucial question: Do you have the guts? Though it may seem that cyclical investing is easy, it certainly isn't. It may be that the stock price trends are reasonably predictable, but even so cyclical stocks can move very quickly. Before you realize it, you're left out in the cold.

Not only that, you have to be very confident in your own predictions about the economy and industrial trends. It's only by thinking independently that you can really succeed. If you invest *after* clear signs of the new cycle are available, you risk missing out on most of the move in your stocks. That's because stocks tend to anticipate the economic cycles.

Rebound on the Horizon

Often you have to act against the prevailing wisdom. If economists are trashing the economy and analysts are predicting dire times ahead for stocks, you might very well see things differently and be in there buying. You may believe that those pessimistic views merely mean that things can't get any worse and that a rebound is on the horizon for both the economy and stock market.

Peter Lynch said it best in his book *One Up on Wall Street*: "Timing is everything in cyclicals, and you have to be able to detect the early signs that business is falling off or picking up. If you work in some profession that's connected to steel, aluminum, airlines, automobiles, etc., then you've got your edge, and nowhere is it more important than in this kind of investment."

It may seem that in cyclical investing you just come up with the trend and then indiscriminately buy stocks that will benefit. Nothing could be further from the truth. Though the big picture does play its important part, it's still crucial to study your stock picks on an individual basis. The stronger the company the better it will weather the economic downturns and the more it will shine when the economy improves.

Cyclical stocks also present some great value opportunities. After these stocks get battered amid a slumping economy, it's always a good idea to take a close look at the company's fundamentals. Has the stock gotten beaten down more than the numbers justify? In other words, is the stock price now below the true worth of the company? You'll find that earnings of some cyclicals aren't nearly as adversely affected by a downturn in the economy as the plunge in the stock price would imply. Often the price gets caught up in the sweep of investors' emotions. That sets up a classic value situation that a savvy investor should always be on the lookout for.

A warning, however: Don't mistake a strong cyclical stock for a growth stock that seems a good value. Some cyclical stocks may appear by some measurements to be great buys; they may look like they're producing fabulous earnings and selling at a decent price. It may seem that their earnings will continue to be terrific for some time; you could be deceived into believing this stock is just like a growth stock with its consistently strong earnings. But the reason the cyclical looks so good is that it's probably near the top of its cycle. Its earnings are so good that even though its stock price has climbed, too, it still has a decent P/E ratio.

Goodyear Goes Flat

Consider Goodyear Tire. In 1987, the company looked very strong. If you measured the stock in terms of its growth-to-P/E ratio, you would have come up with a very attractive 2.4. At the time, Goodyear's earnings were growing at a strong 20% a year and the stock was selling at a decent P/E ratio of 8.3. But that measure—growth-to-P/E ratio—is more suited for measuring growth stocks than cyclicals. If you had used it to analyze the prospects of a cyclical like Goodyear, you would have been sorry.

Since Goodyear's cycle was indeed at its peak in 1987, the stock subsequently fell on hard times. It sank from a high of $38.30 in 1987 to a low of $6.40 in 1990. At the same time, earnings declined from a high of $3.64 a share in 1987 to 33 cents a share in 1990.

But was Goodyear—as a true cyclical stock—a good buy at its low in 1990? The answer is a definite yes. How would you know? If you look at the right measurements for a cyclical stock, you find value. For instance, Goodyear's book value in 1990 was about $18 a share, while its stock price was $6.40; that's quite attractive. Not only that, Goodyear was paying a dividend of 90 cents a share, which works out to a huge dividend yield of 14%. Even though the company slashed dividends the following year, the number still shows how cheap the stock was in 1990. In addition, the company's cash flow per share was $3.22 for a price-to-cash flow of about two to one. That screams out the stock's attractiveness.

So did Goodyear prove to be a good buy in 1990? I wish I'd been

Hitting the Skids

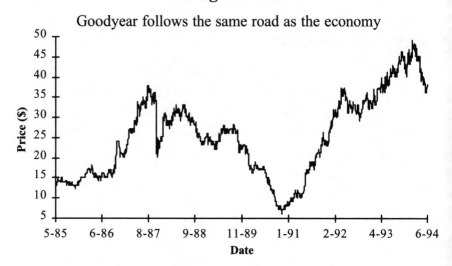

Goodyear follows the same road as the economy

in it. The stock climbed from $6.30 a share to $38 by mid-1992, a 600% gain in two years.

What all this shows is that when assessing any stock, be careful. Just applying the formulas isn't enough. You need to think things through: if cyclicals go through cycles, where are they in their cycles? And if you are looking for true value, use the appropriate value measurements.

Housing the Hovnanian Way

If you know where the economy is in its ever-changing cycle, you will probably know how the home building industry is faring. Home builders are extremely sensitive to the ups and downs of the economy. It's not hard to understand why.

In the first place, buying a home is a major purchase—often the biggest one a family makes. So if the economy isn't doing great, and if your job looks threatened, you're less likely to take the giant plunge into home owning. Therefore, a weak economy equals lackluster business for home builders. Likewise, if the economy is humming and you're getting fat pay raises and your job looks secure, chances are you'll be more inclined to risk a huge investment in a house.

Interest rates also affect home buying. Since most everyone takes out a mortgage to purchase a house, the interest rate on the mortgage tends to spur or inhibit sales. Higher rates translate into higher mortgage payments, so potential home buyers may hesitate. Lower rates reduce mortgage costs, encouraging home sales.

But there's a catch. Often when rates are attractively low for consumers, the economy is sluggish. Low interest rates are an advertisement to consumers that the economy needs their help to get going again. The Federal Reserve will lower rates in times of economic malaise in the hopes that borrowing will pick up and spur economic activity. Similarly, rates are often high when the economy is humming, pushed higher in an effort to prevent an overheating. Interest rates provide a window on the cycles of the economy. But it's never easy knowing when they can't go any lower or any higher. Not only that, predicting the economic cycles based on trends in interest rates is an imprecise science at best. The greatest economic minds wind up baffled by the effort.

Nonetheless, interest rates remain a powerful engine driving the economic cycles. And it pays to understand their implications as best you can. Housing offers a good illustration of how the pieces come together. If rates are low because the economy is at or near its low point in the cycle, some consumers may want to chance a home purchase in anticipation of the stronger economy and to take advantage of the low rates while they can. If rates are high because the economy is heading toward its peak in the cycle, consumers may want to wait for a bit of cooling and a decline in rates before they buy. Again, it's impossible to know where the highs and lows are but it's essential to understand how the economic cycles unfold.

Home builders like Hovnanian Enterprises know all too well the impact of a change in rates and in the economic winds. Hovnanian builds condominiums, townhouses, and single-family homes in planned communities. Its properties are moderately priced for first- and second-time buyers.

In the middle and late 1980s, Hovnanian was on a roll. Thanks to a strong economy and a good housing market, the company prospered. It didn't hurt that Hovnanian also was well managed and offered nice properties. Indeed, they could barely build their homes fast enough for consumers' voracious appetites. In 1989, the company earned $28.8 million, a 512% gain from the $4.7 million profit in 1984.

But hard times lay just ahead. The economy slumped into a recession in the early 1990s, dragging the real estate market into the doldrums. The flood of Hovnanian customers slowed to a trickle, and earnings plunged. From a high of $1.26 a share in 1988, profits disappeared entirely by 1990 when the company recorded a loss of 74 cents a share.

The stock price especially felt the squeeze. It sank from $12 a share in 1989 to a low of $2 in 1990.

In truly cyclical fashion, however, the company bounced back as the economy regained its footing. Hovnanian returned to profitability in 1991, with earnings of seven cents a share. In 1992, profits grew to 43 cents a share and then nearly doubled to 82 cents in 1993.

And look at that stock price! From its low of $2 a share in 1990, Hovnanian climbed to $16 in 1992 for about an 800% gain in two years.

Could you have identified Hovnanian as a good stock prospect amid its lows in 1990? First, if you were attuned to economic cycles you might have been rooting around among the economically sensitive stocks like the home builders for some good values. Second, if you had looked at Hovnanian's book value at the time, you probably would have seen something you liked. In 1990, its book value was more than $6 a share, while its stock price was a mere $2. That would have told you that you were getting a lot of company for the price.

If you like the idea of investing in cyclicals, it's always a good idea to study various stocks within the same industry. It's true that similar industry stocks will move in tandem with the economic cycles. But on close investigation some companies will prove to be better prospects than others.

Cyclical Stocks Mirror the Economy

Home builders Hovnanian, Toll Brothers, and Del Webb soar in the roaring
1980s and fall back to earth in the recession of the early 1990s

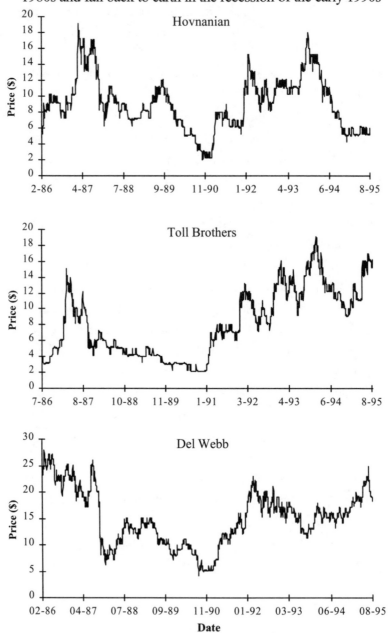

INVESTING IN TURNAROUNDS

Turnarounds offer the potential for a big gain in a short time. But with possible rewards come substantial risks. These situations are among the hardest to get right.

A potential turnaround company is one that isn't just suffering a slowdown: It's actually the pits. At first glance, it looks awful; it may be in bankruptcy or very close to it. In any case, something is really messed up. For the company, things are about as lousy as they get.

So you have to ask: "Why would you expect this dog of a company to turn around?" That's the key. If you can answer that question correctly, you have a chance of cashing in.

There are a variety of reasons a company suffers a terrible change in its fortunes. Sometimes the market for its products changes and the company fails to keep pace. Remember what happened to IBM. The technology wave spurred growth in personal computers when IBM was banking on mainframes continuing to carry the day. Or consider the woes of the defense industry. When the government cut back on military spending, defense companies couldn't help suffering. Some companies go into a tailspin because management makes some stupid decisions or is just inept.

Any material change from these sorry circumstances tags the dog for a possible reversal of fortune. In IBM's case, it was a matter of catching up to the trends *and* installing new management. Under Chairman and Chief Executive Officer Louis V. Gerstner, IBM has refocused and become more efficient through a change in its corporate culture and some layoffs.

In the defense industry, some companies effected turnarounds by retooling to produce new products or by adapting their products and technology to the nonmilitary consumer. Now companies like

Rockwell International are selling modems, auto parts, and commercial aviation electronics rather than B-1 bombers, Hellfire tactical missiles, and space shuttles.

As with cyclicals, it takes guts to bet on a turnaround. To prosper, you have to buy the companies when they're at their worst. When everybody is writing them off, calling them all sorts of bad names, and saying there's basically no hope, that's when you have to drum up your courage and buy the stock. A tipoff that a company is at its lowest point is when you hear analysts complaining about any revival effort as "too little, too late."

The Snowball Effect

But don't expect every company that's flat on its back to resurrect itself. The real risk is whether it can. More often than not, companies that get beaten into the ground have a hard time getting back on their feet. Troubles often snowball. Believe me, a lot of companies go bankrupt in the United State and instead of bouncing back they disappear.

You can also find yourself clinging to false hopes. Every time a company starts to sink, there's talk of big changes. That may tickle investors' interest. The company may begin laying off workers to cut costs, and may bring in new management who talks a good line about repairing the damage. But, in fact, sometimes it is "too little, too late." Sure, a lot of turnarounds wind up being successful, but a lot of them fail, too.

If you like the idea of investing in turnarounds, all I can say is that you mostly have to put your faith in management. But we've already discussed how difficult it is to evaluate management, and it's made all the harder with a turnaround because you don't have any good products to assess as a sign of management's expertise.

What's more, my process for identifying good stock picks isn't a lot of help with turnarounds. Sure, you can rely on your instincts— but that's about all you'll have. The numbers you'd want to analyze in a turnaround will probably look terrible. Everywhere you turn you're likely to see red flags. You'll probably see poor earnings and a lot of debt.

Yet for some reason, many investors are enchanted by turna- rounds. These situations seem to touch something in investors' souls. The problem is that investors get dangerously attached to a potential turnaround. The stocks are usually pretty cheap and in- vestors see more hope than any reality about the company. I think it has something to do with the idea of rooting for the underdog. Americans in particular love the notion that no matter how bleak things look, it is still possible to snatch victory out of the jaws of defeat.

I don't buy it. Though there's a lot of money to be made if you get it right, I'd rather go with a more sure bet based on solid anal- ysis.

The Resurrection of American Express

Consider the case of American Express. Here's the perfect example of a terrific turnaround. It also serves as a perfect illustration of why it's so hard to pick a winning turnaround situation.

Everybody knows the greatness of American Express. A true global powerhouse, the company had enjoyed twenty-three straight years of record operating profits by 1970. It invented the traveler's checks industry. Its credit card was a symbol of prestige. If you could flash a green Amex card, you'd made it; the next symbol of success became Amex's gold and platinum cards.

Those were the glory days of the 1980s. It was the era of image, and American Express was something of an arbiter of status. Then the 1990s rolled around. The new decade brought recession. Not only that, in the 1990s people began to reject the excesses of the 1980s—those go-go years of high debt and high glamour.

American Express fared poorly in the new era. In the recession of the early 1990s, many people found themselves jobless, and they were forced to cut back on their spending. Worst of all for American Express, they trimmed their use of credit cards to chip away at their high personal debt levels.

In 1992, American Express was facing big, nearly insoluable problems for the first time in its history. The future looked uncertain.

Even American Express's great new product, the Optima card, was flagging. Optima, an ordinary credit card, was a departure from the usual American Express charge cards whose balances had to be settled in full each month. It was aimed at the average credit card user who preferred paying off his bills in installments with a finance fee tacked on.

But many users of other credit cards didn't find any reason to switch to the American Express card. And a number who did were defaulting on their Optima debt.

If the credit card troubles weren't enough, the American Express subsidiary Shearson Lehman Brothers was sinking into the red. In 1992, the brokerage company lost $116 million.

Simply put, a mountain of trouble was wreaking havoc on the American Express balance sheet. Earnings hit a low of $1.30 per share in 1992, down from a high of $2.30 a share in 1989. The company's debt-to-equity ratio stood at a dangerously high 2.16; in other words, debt was more than two times equity when it should be only about a quarter of equity. The return on equity slid to a mere 5.7%. A good figure for return on equity is 35%, and anything below 15% is pretty suspect.

The turnaround was initiated in 1993. That's when Harvey Golub moved in as chief executive officer, replacing the much maligned James Robinson III. His task was to cut costs and put American Express on a new course. Among other moves, he jettisoned the Shearson Lehman unit, picking up $1 billion from the sale to Primerica. The funds helped repay debt and fortify the balance sheet.

He also focused on revitalizing the Optima card business. He tried to cut down on high-risk card users by tightening controls on applicants. He set up some perks to lure customers to the card, and he cut the charges American Express demands of merchants who accept the card. Reducing those charges helped persuade more merchants to honor Optima cards. Optima is still losing money but things are looking up.

In addition, he cut costs at American Express's Travel Related Services, the credit card division, by laying off 4,800 workers, or 9% of the staff.

How Golub Gladdens Shareholders

The success of all these moves jumps out at you in the company's financial statements and in its stock price. Clearly, American Express shareholders are glad Golub came around. In 1993, the company's earnings rose 75% from the year earlier to $2.30 a share. Net profit margins also improved dramatically, climbing to 8.3% in 1993 from a mere 2.4% in 1992. The debt-to-equity ratio shrank to 1.04 in 1993 from 2.16 in 1992, still not terribly attractive but at least a drastic improvement. Return on equity also jumped to 20.5% in 1993 from the paltry 5.7% in 1992.

Investors piled back into the stock. In late 1993, American Express hit a high of $36.60, an 83% gain from its $20 level in 1992.

Overall, American Express looks like it was a pretty easy call—

everybody could see it was a winning situation.

Ha! Forget that idea.

That's just Monday morning quarterbacking.

Of course, now it's easy to say that American Express looked like a sure bet. Everything is easy in hindsight.

But there was nothing I saw at the time that convinced me this stock offered any hope of big gains. Indeed, if I had studied the company with my disciplined eye—carefully applying my process— I would have run away from American Express as fast as I could. From an anecdotal point of view, I saw that a lot of people weren't using their American Express cards. Subjectively, I felt the trend was against the company.

Suppose I ruled out the first step in my process. If I had ignored my subjective view and gone directly to the numbers, I still wouldn't have found anything to excite me. An analysis of American Express's numbers in 1992 suggested that the future promised only dismal returns. The stock, though it already had sunk, looked ready to fall still further.

So how *could* anyone see bright prospects in the company back in 1992? My only answer is that you would have had to know the company's operations intimately. Perhaps you knew people who worked there, and they said things weren't really as bad as they appeared. Also, you might have taken the risky approach of putting your faith in the new management. After all, it was Golub who did turn the company around. But, as I've said, it's always difficult to assess the likely success of management. I suppose if you were good friends with Golub or knew him and his abilities, you might have been willing to bet on his success.

Despite everything I've said, I *can* actually claim to have picked American Express as a good turnaround prospect—though I'd be lying if I said I did it based on anything other than a little luck and a smart mouth.

One day back in 1992 my dad and I were discussing the woes of American Express. He asserted that there was no way the company could ever come back. "It's going down," he predicted.

Just to be contradictory, I disagreed. I insisted that American Express would indeed recover. Lo and behold, I was right.

I mention this not just to crow. There's a lesson to be learned: It never hurts to be a contrarian. Or put another way, there's a lot to be gained if you think independently.

Chrysler Magic

Most companies are lucky to bounce back from the brink even once. Chrysler has the dubious distinction of coming back from the dead twice.

Was it easy to recognize that Chrysler would succeed in making its turnarounds? Hardly. Each time, the prognosis looked bleak for America's number three automaker. If you listened to the naysayers, you wouldn't have gone near the stock. At the same time, a look at the company's fundamentals wasn't terribly encouraging. So Chrysler also presented a stock investor with a tough and risky decision.

In hindsight (or again, with the clear vision of the Monday morning quarterback), Chrysler's revival in the 1980s is regarded as probably the greatest turnaround ever. As everyone knows, the company was on its knees and about to topple. The economy was weak, car purchases were slow, and if consumers did buy, they weren't choosing Chrysler. To make matters worse, Chrysler's costs of producing cars were the highest in the industry. And the higher expenses weren't reflected in the quality: the cars coming off the assembly line were pretty crummy.

Enter Lee Iacocca. His arrival as chairman shook Chrysler out of its stupor. He reorganized management, ridding the company of

Turnaround Heaven

American Express pays off handsomely for investors who bet on the company's revival

what he saw as anarchy. He vigorously attacked the problem of high costs. He shut down factories and revamped Chrysler's production process. A new line of cars and the introduction of minivans were designed to take the company around the corner to recovery.

Of course, as everyone knows, Iacocca had a little help. None of his efforts would have been possible without a government bailout for the company. In 1980, Chrysler got a $1.5 billion loan from the U.S. coffers. The rescue package helped Chrysler offset its $3.3 billion in losses between 1979 and 1981. By 1983, the company managed to post a profit, emerging from its toughest phase of the turnaround.

The rebirth was amply rewarded in Chrysler's stock price. At its low in the early 1980s, Chrysler was selling at less than $3 a share. By 1987, it hit a peak of $106.80 a share, adjusted for splits. That's a cool 3,560% gain in about six years.

Not bad.

But would you have had the guts to jump into the stock? Even though it performed magnificently, if you had kept a close eye on the company you might not have become all that enamored. In fact, Chrysler wasn't terribly well managed through the 1980s. The company made a few poorly advised acquisitions that cost a lot of time and money. For instance, Chrysler bought four rental car companies: Dollar, General, Snappy, and Thrifty, all of which were still losing money in 1992. Not only that, the design and quality of Chrysler cars didn't improve very much; in fact, they didn't really keep up with the times.

So it was that Chrysler faced its second crisis in a decade. Admittedly, the company's second turnaround didn't come from such a scary bottom as the first. But nonetheless people again began talking about the company vanishing. The media reported in 1991 that Chrysler was on life support.

Indeed, the numbers paint a pretty sorry picture. Earnings hit a peak of $6.31 a share in 1986 and then began shrinking. In 1989, Chrysler earned $1.31 a share; in 1990, profit was a meager 30 cents a share. Then in 1991, the company went into the red again, losing $795 million. The balance sheet looked pretty ugly, too. The company's debt-to-equity ratio remained high, and the return on equity was on a downward spiral, sliding to 4.3% in 1989 and to 1% in 1990. Cyclical stocks typically have a low return on equity at the troughs of their cycles. The poor numbers underscore the weakness of the companies at those times. Remember, under normal circumstances, you want a return on equity of at least 10% to 15%.

Chrysler's credit picture darkened. Both Standard & Poor's and Moody's lowered the company's credit rating, labeling Chrysler's debt as junk. That meant that Chrysler's bonds were riskier and more expensive for investors and that it was harder for the automaker to raise money.

Meanwhile, its market share in the U.S. continued to decline. By 1991, the number three automaker had less than 10% of the U.S. car market. Honda was selling more cars in America in 1991 than Chrysler was.

In 1992, the tide changed. Again, the shift was brought about largely by massive cost cutting and improvements in the way Chrysler cars were produced. The company sharpened efficiency and even began turning out some very good cars.

The cost reduction efforts cost quite a few people their jobs. To save about $660 million a year, Chrysler reduced its rosters by 15,800 workers. Despite less manpower, the company was able to speed up operations.

Other changes aimed at improving the design process and communication among engineers helped cut expenses and reduce costly errors. The company also raised cash in a variety of ways, including selling a stake in Mitsubishi, cutting its dividend, and launching a new stock offering.

The money was spent in the right ways. Chrysler built a $1 billion technical center to push development to new horizons.

All these measures would have been for nothing if Chrysler hadn't come up with some winning models. A car maker without good cars goes nowhere no matter how low its costs or how great its management or how huge its stockpile of cash.

Chrysler's new line of cars did for the company in the 1990s what the government did in the 1980s—laid the groundwork for a viable turnaround. Among the models that proved successful both with consumers and the media were the Dodge Intrepid, Eagle Vision, Chrysler Concorde, and the Jeep Grand Cherokee.

Chrysler led the Big Three automakers out of the recession in the early 1990s, becoming the first to return to the black. And its market share grew. The company earned $477.9 million in 1992; in 1993, its profit grew to $2.415 billion, or $6.77 per share. Its return on equity also looked good at 33.5% in 1993.

And what about the stock price? If you had had the stomach to hold on, you would have patted yourself vigorously on the back. Chrysler's stock slumped to a low of about $9 in 1991, then rebounded to a high of $63.50 in 1994. That's more than a 600% gain.

CHAPTER SIXTEEN

Catch the Wave:
Betting on Technology

Bye-bye, Buffett

When it comes to technology stocks, I bid adieu to my heroes. Neither Warren Buffett nor Peter Lynch is a big fan of technology. I, however, love the sector. The group represents an unbelievable moneymaking opportunity. And a pretty easy one, too.

I don't remember Warren Buffett ever saying anything outright about a technology stock but neither can I recall an instance where he actually bought one. Peter Lynch's aversion to the sector was more direct. His first book, *One Up on Wall Street* seemed to me to be a giant red flag screaming: "Invest in Technology, Lose Your Wallet!"

For all my admiration of these men, you can't escape the fact that they are products of an earlier generation. Their advice that you should invest in what you know is sound. But for them, the technology revolution came a little too late. They may be somewhat afraid of it.

Of course, not everyone of the earlier generation shunned

technology. One of the greatest investors of all time, Philip Fisher, was a technology aficionado long before anyone ever heard of Microsoft. And he's of an earlier generation than either Buffett or Lynch.

Fisher's discovery of technology was due partly to sharp insight and partly to his surroundings. He went to business school at Stanford University and started his own investment counseling firm, Fisher & Company, in 1931. Motorola was one of his early technology picks. He also recommended and bought shares of Texas Instruments in the 1950s. He held on to that stock for decades and made a bundle. His wisdom on investing in general is contained in his famous book *Common Stocks and Uncommon Profits*.

His decision to include technology stocks in his portfolio is especially remarkable because of the developing state of the industry at the time. If technology seems arcane these days, back then few people outside the technical world had any handle on it at all. At least today the average person can get loads of information about technology and educate himself pretty easily; when Fisher was first buying technology stocks not nearly as much information was available. If you weren't a technician, you had to forget about understanding anything. And Fisher was no technician.

But he *did* have an advantage. He grew up, lived, and worked next door to California's Silicon Valley, where many technological innovations were born. John Train in *The Money Masters* credits Fisher's surroundings as key to his understanding of technology.

There's a lot of truth to that. The more you are surrounded by something the better you can understand it. Since technology is so prevalent today, it's a lot easier to understand.

Especially for people of my generation. Generation X practically eats computer chips for breakfast. We can tell you the best chip manufacturer just as easily as Peter Lynch can tell you the best maker of that old breakfast cereal, cornflakes. Even though Peter

Lynch and Warren Buffet in many respects have been exposed to technology just as much as I have been, they were already well into their careers and their investment biases were set by the time the technorevolution struck.

Their caution about the sector is understandable. There are many investors out there who view technology as a sure bet. These types invest blindly, expecting the great technological era to make them rich no matter what. Poor fools.

I've witnessed this blindness among some of the regulars at my local Schwab office. Somebody comes up to me and gushes about a great new tech stock he just bought, trying to get me to buy the same one. I ask a few questions such as, what about the competition, the stock's price-to-earnings ratio, new products? And they look at me and say, "Gee, I dunno."

That attitude is the surest way to see your money disappear into cyberspace.

Technology is very complicated these days. There is a lot to learn. If you attempt to profit from its great potential, you have to think carefully about the sector. In the first place, you can't think of technology as just one giant clump of similar stocks. There are many differences within the sector.

I break the group down into four fairly distinct areas: software, telecommunications, semiconductors, and computers. Each of these is really an industry by itself, and each plays a special and important role.

Welcome to the Future

When people think about technology, they often picture a scene from *The Jetsons* in which everyone is buzzing around in private spaceships. There is something to that image. Technology conjures up all sorts of fantastic ideas and they all point in one direction: the future. There's now even a common belief that technology is almost synonymous with the future. The word itself excites the imagination.

But for all the wonder and hype surrounding technology it's important to keep your feet firmly planted in the here and now. Sure, there's great promise. But there are also great failures ahead. As anyone knows, the path to the future is not a straight line. As stock investors, you mustn't lose a sense of reality about technology. You must study the stocks with the same consideration as you would any other industry.

Having said that, however, I also want to remind you that with any stock investment a key consideration is the industry the company operates in. You're looking for growth. In my view, there are few industries with the growth potential of technology.

Think back to the time when man first took to the air. It was inevitably the dawning of the age of airplanes. If you were an investor then, would you want to pump more money into railroad stocks? Or would you want to take off with the aviation industry? The answer is pretty clear. Future growth looked a lot more promising on the cutting edge than with yesterday's ideas.

So it is with technology.

Think again of the four major industries within technology: software, semiconductors, telecommunications, and computers. Now think of the demand for these industries' products not only from average consumers but also from corporations. It's a recipe for massive growth.

You hear every day about parents putting more and more emphasis on making their kids computer literate. What does that mean for the industry? Of course, it helps sales in the short term. But it also sets the stage for a major shift in the perspective of people in the future. As these kids grow up computer literate, computers and all the rest of technology will be second nature to them. The technology revolution of today will be the commonplace experience of tomorrow. The products of technology inevitably will surround the consumers of tomorrow in a way we can barely imagine today. The result: steady, strong growth for the industry.

As the computer literate generation enters the work place, it will demand an environment designed with the latest technological advancements. Corporations then will make ever greater use of technology, further spurring the growth of the industry.

The Here and Now

But you don't have to wait for the future to profit from investments in technology. The era of technology investment has arrived. Indeed, within the last few years conditions have become excellent for making money in technology stocks. The simple reason is that many of the companies are now very profitable.

That wasn't the case a few decades ago. Only a few companies like IBM were turning a profit. Technology was still a dream then. Many companies held out great hope but hadn't really produced much. In fact, they were probably pretty poor investments back then if you looked at their bottom lines.

Not so today. A horde of technology companies today are not only profitable but are also still facing vast untapped or unsaturated markets. These companies are so profitable right now that consideration of their bright futures can even take a backseat.

Consider Motorola. It's a prime example of a company whose profits are soaring in the present and are pegged to climb further in the future. It's a leading manufacturer of semiconductors and cellular phones.

Motorola's market is still wide open and demand is expected to grow steadily, as everyone ten years from now will have a cellular phone or some kind of semiconductor with them constantly. But that's only a bonus for owning Motorola today.

The fact is the company is so profitable right now than an investor doesn't have to concern himself too much with the distant future.

But, of course, if you're a long-term investor the future is a pretty picture as well.

Beating the Nitwits

There are a lot of nitwits investing in technology. It amazes me to see which investors are betting on the sector and how they do it. Many people who invest in technology haven't taken the time to educate themselves about the special nature of the sector. And so they mess things up for themselves. But if you're a careful, educated investor, you can benefit from the mistakes made by the nitwits.

In essence, the great masses of nitwits are fabulous competition for you. They do all the wrong things—they buy when they shouldn't and they sell when they should hold on. These antics cause the technology sector to be more volatile than other sectors. In their panic, the nitwits drive prices lower than they ought to be, creating great bargains for you, the smart investor. In their enthusiasm, they drive prices higher than they should be, creating great profits for you if you own the same stocks.

You run into nitwit investors in all sectors of the market. But for some reason they seem to be most plentiful in the technology sector. It's partly because technology is subject to such excessive optimism—and excessive pessimism when things go wrong. And it's also because people like to talk off the top of their heads when they don't really know much about a subject.

If you try to pin someone down about why he invests in a certain technology stock, you'll hear a whole range of strange and misguided excuses.

"I dunno," someone will say, "but the stock has been going up faster than my fat sister can eat a cherry pie after fasting."

Or here's an easy one: "It's going to be the next Microsoft."

Sometimes people try to sound learned: "I hear they came up with something that solves a lot of problems."

Often investors don't even know what product the company makes. If you ask the question they'll just slough it off with, "Hey, it's a tech company." It seems good enough just to mention the word "tech."

Ask how the numbers stack up at the company, or even if the company is profitable, and you'll probably be met with a blank stare.

People jump into and fly out of technology stocks often on the slightest rumor. The sector is fed by the swirl of gossip. Since investors are aching to jump on the latest bandwagon, analysts' recommendations also send stocks gyrating. A positive word from Wall Street and the stock soars. Likewise, a negative comment and prices tumble.

The smart investor can take advantage of all the rumors, misinformation, ecstasy, and panic that the technology sector provokes. But to be smart you must follow my three basic principles, especially when you're investing in technology. You risk getting burned worse than with other types of stocks, unless you: 1) educate yourself thoroughly; 2) think independently (beware of bandwagons!); and 3) are logical.

Consider Tseng Labs, a company that develops semiconductors for IBM and IBM-compatible computers. A nitwit and a smart investor probably would have behaved quite differently toward this stock. Look at the chart on page 212. Notice the price movement just from late 1990 to late 1991. See how the stock climbed from $4 to nearly $20 and then fell back to about $10.

The nitwit investor probably would have panicked at the decline and bailed out, fearing some terrible problem with the company. Of course, this investor wouldn't know if anything was wrong or not because he didn't do his homework.

The smart investor, by contrast, would have held on. Notice the wisdom in that. The stock resumed its upward climb, going all the way to nearly $25.

What separated the smart investor from the nitwit? The smart investor knew the company's numbers. He saw that even though the stock was volatile, the earnings growth remained strong. What's more, the P/E ratio also stayed in an attractive range of 12 to 14. Besides, the company had no debt and its return on equity was consistently strong at more than 20%.

Similarly, the educated investor could have benefited from the strength in the stock of software maker Adobe Systems. But again, he would have had to ride out the sharp swings in prices.

The chart on page 212 shows that Adobe has undergone the characteristic volatility of a technology stock. But anyone who studied the company's numbers would have seen that at the low points, the stock presented great value. Here was a company that consistently turned in good earnings and boasted other strong numbers. It had very little debt and showed a return on equity of more than 19%.

Getting Educated

You can learn about hot technology companies by just opening your eyes and looking at all the things surrounding you. Anybody who has looked at various computers either at his own house or friends' houses or in stores has seen the little sticker that says: INTEL INSIDE. It's all over the place.

Turning Volatility into Profits

Price fluctuations of Tseng Labs look scary but really are moneymaking opportunities

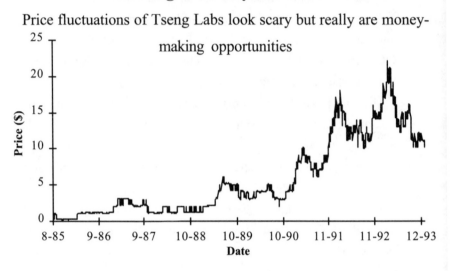

Riding the Technology Stock Roller Coaster

Adobe Systems provides many opportunities to buy low and sell high

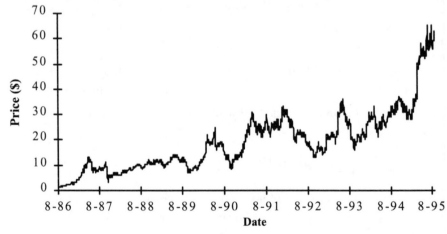

That should set off bells in your head. If you didn't know any-thing about Intel and saw those stickers everywhere, you should be asking yourself, "What is that all about?"

Your answer would have led you to an unbelievably great stock. Intel is a leading manufacturer of integrated circuits for personal computers. That so many of those stickers saying "Intel Inside" appear on so many computers tells you that the company's products are widely used. In turn, that suggests strong earnings. And those earnings suggest a lofty stock price.

And that's been precisely the scenario for Intel. Riding the boom in the personal computer market, the company has more than quad-rupled its earnings to $2.94 a share in 1994 from 63 cents a share in 1988. And what about the stock price? Shareholders are smiling as the price has climbed 1,400% from $5 a share in 1988 to more than $75 a share in 1995, adjusted for splits.

If I had hung around my dad's office a little more than I did, I might not have missed Autodesk. It produces computer-aided de-sign, or CAD, and computer-aided engineering, or CAE, software. It's designed mostly for people in the engineering industry such as draftsmen and designers. This software is to engineers and drafts-men what word processing software is to writers—what was once done manually is now done by computer.

Autodesk's chief product was the first computer-aided design software for desktop personal computers. My dad once told me, "It's quite a package. Everybody uses it."

Here was a product that literally surrounded my dad and people in the engineering business. If I'd opened my eyes a little wider, perhaps I'd have found Autodesk stock in time to ride its superb growth.

Today, it has 70% of the market for computer-aided design soft-ware. Its earnings have grown steadily, from 17 cents a share in 1985 to $1.47 in 1994, adjusted for splits. That's more than an 850%

increase. The stock soared from $3.67 at the time of its initial public offering in 1985 to $44 in 1995, split adjusted, for a gain of nearly 1,100%.

Free Info at the Library

But you can't learn about technology only by opening your eyes to everything around you. You need to research the industry. You need to study it carefully. You need to educate yourself.

People like Warren Buffett shy away from technology because, as he explains it, he doesn't understand the business. Of course, he's right—if you don't understand a business, don't invest in it. But there's no reason you can't learn what's going on in technology.

It was tougher to understand the industry several years ago. There wasn't as much information available as there is today. Most people didn't know very much about the companies and their products. As a result, only investors with intimate knowledge of a company or trends in the industry had any success with technology stocks.

Times are different today. The information is out there for anyone to find. You can win in technology stocks just as easily as the most informed analyst on Wall Street.

Yes, there's great potential here. But at the same time, there's great danger. I'd go so far as to say that to do well in technology, you *have* to research the companies. If you fail to do your homework, you do so at your peril.

The key is simply knowing where to look.

I may have been exposed to computers and the wonders of technology at an early age, but I certainly didn't know nearly enough to make intelligent stock decisions. Now I'm up to speed and can't get enough of technology stocks. How did I make the leap?

Simple.

I got most of my technology education for free right out of the library.

Once when I was waiting for my mom to pick me up, I happened to flip through *PC Week*. I couldn't believe it! Like most people, I thought this magazine was just for technonerds. I was even repelled by the name. Any magazine with the initials PC in the title had to be far too complicated for the average guy, or else a complete bore.

Nothing could be further from the truth. Not only *PC Week* but *PC Magazine, PC World,* and other PC magazines are usually easy to read and full of color and lively illustrations. The average person could pick up one and jump right in.

For anyone interested in technology stocks, these magazines are essential reading. They have the same goal as the stock investor: to stay on top of the latest products and trends.

For instance, when a lot of notebook computers were hitting the market, the magazines did rigorous comparisons of the products. In one of its issues, *PC Computing* tested the notebooks on four criteria: usability, durability, portability, and performance. It looked at the products' memory, speed, and how well they survived hot temperatures, cold temperatures, liquid spills, and drops to the floor. The publication also studied the notebooks through the eyes of the individual consumer and the corporate user. In the end, thirteen notebooks got passing marks. The best among the group was a Dell product, the Latitude XP 4100 CX.

Knowing that Dell ranked top in that magazine survey is one bit of information that a stock investor can put to use. It could spark your interest to research the company more fully. Or it could encourage you about other positive aspects of the company you already knew.

A Software Winner

Combining personal observation and library research can pay off handsomely. Consider my investment in the software company Corel.

I'd never heard of the company until my Canadian markets analyst mentioned it to me. (My Canadian markets analyst is really my cousin William. I don't pay him for his advice; he just offers it. It's the same kind of set-up I have with my auto analyst, who happens to be my good friend John Vincler. William is Canadian and he loves nothing more than to push Canadian stocks on me.) Corel, he insisted, was a great company and its products were fantastic.

I had my doubts but I never reject any stock suggestion outright. So I decided to check it out.

I discovered in *Value Line* and *Standard & Poor's* stock reports that Corel primarily makes graphics software for Microsoft Windows.

My first step was to check out the computer store. I wanted to see Corel's products on the shelf. I wanted to learn what I could just from reading the boxes and talking to people at the store. I just wanted to get a feel for the software, if I could.

Next, I headed to the library. And what I found there blew me away. I punched the company's name in on the InfoTrac computer and studied all the articles written about Corel. I focused on the stories about Corel's software products. InfoTrac lets you single out articles on a range of company subjects—you can get general information or you can zero in on the products.

My eyes got wider with each article I read. Corel's products received very positive evaluations in every case. What's more, measured against other company's products, Corel's software was invariably ranked either near or at the top.

In October 1989, *PC Week* published the results of a poll meas-uring corporate satisfaction with various vector-based drawing packages. The magazine asked respondents to assess certain char-acteristics such as reliability, ease of training and use, and the ac-curacy of the image represented on-screen. Corel's graphics software CorelDRAW was found to provide the highest level of overall satisfaction.

That was just the beginning of Corel's laurels. In September 1990, *PC Magazine* compared five freehand illustration packages. Corel's CorelDRAW and Micrografx's Designer shared top honors. *PC Magazine* also named CorelDRAW version 2.01 the best PC-based illustration software for 1991. In October 1992, *Infoworld* reviewed CorelDRAW 3.0b, commenting that its "simple, almost ideal, in-terface and comprehensive features make this program one of the easiest drawing programs to use and an excellent value." In Sep-tember 1993, *Consumer's Guide Magazine* named CorelDRAW 3.0 a best buy.

The evidence was clearly building, and Corel looked like an ex-cellent prospect. But even though the reviews were uniformly pos-itive, I still wanted to investigate the company a little further. When it comes to a potential stock investment, you can never know too much.

So I talked to a friend who worked part time in a local computer store. He was fascinated by technology and was a computer buff, and I trusted his opinion. He knew a lot more than I did.

I asked him about Corel and its software products. His answers paralleled what I'd read in the library. He pointed out that Corel's was undoubtedly the best-selling software of its kind. He noted that the regulars at the computer store were very satisfied with it, almost to an unexpected degree. Clearly, the company produced a superior product. Overall, he confirmed my suspicion that Corel was an ex-cellent company.

I checked out the company's numbers and was further encouraged to buy the stock. Earnings were pushing consistently upward. In 1989, Corel's earnings per share were 11 cents; by 1994, the figure was 67 cents a share. The stock traded at $2 a share in 1989; by 1994, it hit a high of $17.

I did take the plunge into Corel, though I didn't benefit completely from its strong price run. I bought 200 shares in August 1993 at $8 each. I watched the price shoot up to $12 a share by October and decided to sell. Though the swift climb gave me a fear of heights and I sold too soon, I still walked away with a 50% gain in about two months.

Finding Superior Products

All of your observations and research should ultimately be directed at one primary goal: understanding the company's products. You have to get past the technical mumbo jumbo and figure out what the products actually do. The technical side of technology tends to scare people off; but it's not that difficult to crack if you do your research and ask a lot of questions. Remember there are people whose job it is to answer those questions.

You'll find that truly understanding technology brings immense rewards, both personal and financial. Only with understanding can you assess various products to discover the ones that are superior. If a company doesn't produce a superior product, look elsewhere for an investment.

The simple fact is that superior products lead to superior stocks.

To recognize a superior product you need to analyze the competition. You have to fully understand the competition's product as well as your potential stock pick's. You must ask yourself what makes one product superior to the other, and how close the competitor is to coming up with a rival product.

Keep in mind that even though one product may outsell another, it may not be a superior item. The sales may be spurred by price-cutting or some other gimmick. If a company truly lacks technical superiority, that deficiency will eventually be revealed. The company is in a vulnerable position—and so are investors in its stock.

If you want to see the benefits of product superiority, look no further than the giant software maker Microsoft. It has become the dominant company in its field largely for that one reason—its products put others to shame. Now its Windows application is found on practically every home computer. Its Access, Excel, and Word programs are standards in the industry. Why? Because these database, spreadsheet, and word-processing programs were easier to use than existing ones. Not only that, they are more powerful and technologically superior.

Microsoft stock certainly has rewarded shareholders. It went public in 1986 at $1.17 and sold in 1995 for about $100 a share, adjusted for splits. That's a gain of almost 8,500% in just nine years.

If you know your company's products, you can weather the hurricanes that often blow through the technology sector. If a stock price starts to fall and you're convinced of the company's product superiority, you'll be more likely to hold on and ride it out. If you're right, the stock will bounce back and probably go higher. The knowledgeable investor is able to write off the squalls in technology stocks as just the usual volatility of the sector. Your understanding of the products is like a warm blanket in a horrific storm.

Remember my experience with Chipcom. I watched the stock plunge from $40 a share to $21. Understandably, I panicked. It's just human nature to worry when you see something like that. I was full of doubts about the wisdom of my investment in the company. All I heard was people trashing the stock, predicting it was headed even lower.

But lucky for me, I knew Chipcom. I'd done my homework. I

knew it was a good company, had sound fundamental strength, superior products. I steeled myself and fought my panic. After careful consideration, I decided it was stupid of me to panic at all. In fact, I realized I was staring at a great buying opportunity after the stock's freefall. So I bought some more.

Then I sat back and watched it climb from $21 to $51, adjusted for splits.

Great Idea but . . .

Many people mistakenly believe that a company with a great idea inevitably becomes a company with a great product. Not so. I'd never minimize the importance of ideas but if they're not turned into viable products, they're useless. That's why a fundamental rule for picking technology stocks is to buy an actual product, not an idea.

Nowadays people think almost anything is possible in the technology world. So they jump into stocks of companies that promise unbelievable things. If a company came up with a smartly packaged plan for a machine to clone humans, it could probably sell millions of shares and watch them climb sky-high. Who wouldn't want a gadget like that? Sales would be incredible.

Before you race out and mortgage your house for a bundle of shares, I hope you'd ask yourself: What are the chances of such a machine hitting the market in two years? The proponents might even tell you that seven years is a better time frame. Others might caution that the product won't make its splash for another ten years, or fifty years.

But, of course, you're thinking: If I get into the stock now, just imagine!

I know this is a wild illustration but it's meant to emphasize the point: You're going to be a lot safer with technology investments if you seek superior products rather than the most far out, cutting-edge ideas.

Even if a company is just a year away from launching its product, I'd hesitate to invest. Even if it were a quite viable product that showed considerable promise. The reason is that you really never know what'll happen between now and a year from now. Speculation will run rampant. One week everybody will be cheering the thing as the greatest invention of all times. The next week the product will be seen as the next great flop on the scale of the Edsel.

My advice is to wait for the birth of the product, watch it mature a little and, if it shows greatness without any ifs, ands, or buts, swoop in and buy a load of shares.

To understand the perils, look what happened to the stock of 3DO, a maker of video game systems. This was regarded as one of the hot emerging companies in California's high-tech Silicon Valley.

The company launched a share offering in 1993, even though they had no product to sell. But everyone thought they had great potential. The chairman of another hot company, Electronic Arts, left his firm to set up 3DO. AT&T thought enough of the company to pump money into it. The stock price soared right from the start, climbing as high as $48.

Two months after its shares began trading, 3DO unveiled its first product. It was a video game machine that cost $700. Think about it: $700 for a video game system when you could get a good personal computer for $1,200. And everybody knows a PC does a lot more than just play video games.

Here was a product that saw good hype. It was, in fact, not a bad product. The problem was it just didn't have a place at that price in the market.

Was it any surprise that 3DO stock plummeted from its $48 level to as low as $11.75?

Promises, Promises

3DO shoots up on enthusiasm about its great new video-game machine
then tumbles when the device doesn't live up to expectations

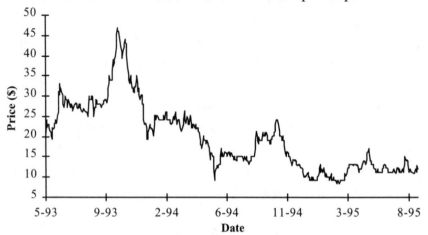

The Bigger Picture

Besides product superiority, you need to keep an eye on larger developments in the industry. Is the field moving in a new direction that may make your company's product obsolete? Even if not, will changes in the industry shrink the market for your company's product? Or is the company poised to capitalize on the latest moves?

If you regularly read the computer magazines a few years ago, you couldn't help noticing a trend that had a strong impact on certain companies and their stock prices. Even the average reader easily would have noticed that the industry was moving away from mainframe computers to personal computers. Who wins and who loses in a major shift like that?

The answer was soon all over the stock pages as IBM's price headed downhill for months, giving many investors a case of the Big Blues. IBM was slow to respond to the shift and continued to rely heavily on mainframe sales. But as personal computers boosted their capabilities they became a cheaper alternative for many companies, not to mention their popularity inside the American home.

If IBM was a loser in the trend, there had to be a few winners. While several PC makers took off, one that stood out was the same company mentioned earlier as a good notebook computer maker: Dell.

Anyone who was careful in his reading and research would have noticed that Dell was a good-looking prospect as an investment. Indeed, amid the changes in the computer industry as mainframes gave way to personal computers and notebooks began to emerge, Dell stock has performed fabulously well. The company went public in 1988 at $5.67. With the help of strong rallies in the past couple of years, the stock was trading in 1995 at around $75 a share. That's a gain of more than 1,200%.

Tallying Up the Numbers

Given the volatility of the technology sector, your analysis of a company's numbers is all the more important. Amid a sharp decline in a stock price, you want to be assured that everything is okay. Your chief assurance lies in the company's numbers. If they're okay, you're okay.

Some people are inclined to overlook the fact that the technology company they're interested in isn't yet profitable. That's a mistake. Sure, technology is a forward-looking industry, but one of the here and now essentials is that the company has a profit before you invest.

You should approach technology investing with the viewpoint of a growth stock investor. And a cardinal element of a growth stock is its earnings: Profits must be growing at a faster rate than other companies' and must be pegged to continue their rapid rate of increase.

If you aren't turning any profit at all, it's hard to show a growth in profit. If a company does suddenly make a profit after losing money, all it has done is go from the red into the black. The idea of growth stocks is to pile up growth on top of growth.

You also should never think of a young technology stock as a turnaround possibility. If a company is having trouble, you'd be better off to ignore it. It's hard enough to pull off a turnaround in any other industry; in technology it's even harder because of the fast-paced nature of change. A company that is simply trying to get on its feet isn't going to have the wherewithal to keep up and compete effectively in that environment, if it does manage to survive.

In the early 1990s, investors fell in love with biotechnology stocks.

There was a lot of media hype about the revolutionary advances in genetic research. Small companies sprang up, hoping to bring new biotech drugs to market and make a killing. Many biotech stocks soared.

But then everyone began to realize that almost none of these companies was making any profit at all. In many cases, the products were still in development or in early stages of clinical testing. Now and then, you'd hear that a miraculous new drug failed to live up to its billing in human tests and the company's stock would plunge.

Investors eventually became less willing to ride on the promise without the proof and the profits. Biotech stocks lost some of their fascination and the group underwent a wrenching readjustment. Many investors ended up sorely disappointed.

Other numbers that technology investors should investigate closely are the company's cash and debt levels. Technology companies need to be constantly improving on their products; they have to push ahead with innovation. That takes cash.

What's more, these companies need to be spending on research and development rather than on paying off their debt. So companies with a lot of debt are at a disadvantage—crucial resources are being funneled in the wrong direction. In other industries, a low debt level is essential for success; in technology, it's even more important. A technology company should be able to finance growth with its own funds or from the sale of its products. When it does start to borrow money, that may be a sign of trouble.

Wait for Your Price

Your final consideration in buying a technology stock is its price. Since a lot of hype about the future infects the industry, many technology stocks sell far above what they're worth. If anyone ever tells you, "No price is too high" for a given stock, turn tail and run. The stock is clearly overpriced.

Among the key numbers to study is the earnings growth-to-P/E ratio. Since earnings often define the attractiveness of a stock, it is useful to measure those earnings against the stock price. In that way, you can determine whether the company offers a value for the amount of earnings it has.

The stock price to research also is worth a serious look. This ratio gives you a window on how seriously the company takes its research and development efforts. A ratio that shows the stock price to be much above the research outlays should raise a warning flag.

Fortunately, technology stocks fluctuate. So if you have analyzed a company thoroughly and determined it's something you want to own, there's a good chance it will get beaten down to a reasonable price. You must be careful to buy technology stocks that show definite value. Usually, just waiting a little while will bring your targeted stock down into the price range you prefer. If it's truly a great company, you can ride it back up.

To get a good price, you must assert your independence of mind. Many times, a stock will climb and everyone will jump in, fearing they'll be left behind. Often, they wind up with a good stock but at a high price. If you ignore the crowd, you may be able to get the same good stock a little later at a much better price. That's after it has risen far too much far too fast and flutters back down to a realistic level.

The price swings may be scary. But don't forget, in technology, they're completely normal. You can use them to your advantage.

CHAPTER SEVENTEEN

Everybody Is
a Kid at Heart

One of the hottest notions in investing right now is that everybody should approach the stock market through the eyes of a kid. Peter Lynch highlighted the idea in his book *Beating the Street,* when he praised the phenomenally successful performance of a seventh-grade class whose mock portfolio gained 70% over two years. Lynch said, "Never invest in any idea you can't illustrate without a crayon."

There's a lot of truth to what Lynch says. Kids *do* naturally have a clearer investment eye than many adults. That's primarily because we haven't ridden the roller coaster that most investors have. We haven't spent the past decade or two or three scouring the stock pages having our hearts rise and fall with every tremor in the market. And, we haven't spent time and money listening to analysts and brokers and financial advisers spew the advice that gets everyone confused and panicky. Instead, we've spent our short lives testing new computers, shopping for the latest electronics, and figuring out what the best sneakers are every year.

So, it makes sense that kids can easily pick out winning stocks such as Mattel and Toys "Я" Us. But don't worry, you don't need to jump into the body of a teenager for your investments to turn out rosy. Kids' great ability to pick stocks doesn't really say anything special about a particular kid talent. People who noticed those stocks merely had their eyes open. And, as I've said throughout this book, adults have the same talent—plus the added advantage of years of life experience looking at the world around them—for picking stocks. Business people can just as easily choose prospective winning stocks among office-machine makers, software companies, airlines, even manufacturers of coffee pots, as the kid who plays computer games and hangs out at Best Buy. For instance, my dad, the engineer, could have seen that Autodesk's drafting software might make that company into a profitable stock pick.

The point is that it doesn't matter if you're a kid or an adult. To succeed in the stock market, you just need to be yourself. What you see in your daily drive to the office or walk to school is filtered through your unique perspective, and it is that original vision of what people are buying, doing, and thinking that you can apply to all of your investment decisions. Everyone can keep his or her eyes open: Look to see which stores are crowded, listen to friends, ask relatives questions about their businesses. It does not end there, though. Then you need to put what you know as an individual consumer together with the financial numbers. You need to do your homework.

The most important principle, however, is the one that calls for you to think independently.

Glossary

Asset allocation: Spreading investments over a variety of categories, with the aim being to maximize returns and minimize volatility.

Balance sheet: A summary of a company's assets, liabilities, and shareholders' equity at a given date.

Book value: A company's worth based on all its assets, minus liabilities and intangibles such as innovation. Generally, what the company would be worth on liquidation. To derive book value per share, subtract liabilities from assets and divide by the number of common shares outstanding. A stock may be selling at a good price when book value is higher than the price of shares.

Bottom-up investing: Investing based on the prospects of individual companies rather than on broad stock market and economic trends. See also TOP-DOWN INVESTING.

Cash flow: The amount of money a company generates from its business. Used to fuel operations, pay dividends, and finance future growth. A good growth indicator and measure of stock value when expressed as a ratio to stock price. The standard cash-to-price ratio is 10 to 1. The higher the cash flow per share, the better value the stock.

Contrarian investing: Investing based on the view that pessimism about the broad market or individual stocks signals an imminent rise in prices. A common contrarian strategy is to sell when large numbers of people are buying and to buy when large numbers of people are selling. See also SHORT INTEREST.

Cyclical stock: A stock that rises and falls in response to economic cycles. A strong economy improves earnings and lifts a cyclical stock, while a weak economy slows earnings and depresses a cyclical stock. Such stocks include autos, home building, clothing, chemicals, steel, and paper.

Debt-to equity ratio: Measures debt in relation to stockholders' equity. The average ratio is at least 1 to 4, or 25%. Debt levels may vary considerably from one industry to another, but in general low debt levels increase a company's attractiveness.

Diversification: Investment in several categories of investment vehicles—such as stocks, bonds, and money market instruments, or a mutual fund—to reduce volatility. See also ASSET ALLOCATION.

Dividend: The amount paid at the discretion of management to shareholders as a share of company profits.

Dividend yield: Rate of return paid to shareholders in dividends, expressed as a percentage of the share price. A $10 stock offering a $2 annual dividend per share would have a yield of 20%.

Dollar cost averaging: Buying stock at set intervals over the long term without regard to share price movement. Since the investor purchases more shares when the price falls and fewer when the price rises, the average share cost to the investor will be lower than the average share cost on the stock exchange during the same time period.

Dow Jones Industrial Average: An index that tracks the price-weighted average of thirty widely held blue-chip stocks traded on the New York Stock Exchange.

Earnings per share: A company's net income divided by the number of shares outstanding.

Growth stock: The stock of a company that demonstrates consistently strong earnings regardless of economic cycles. Though prices may fluctuate wildly and be higher than those of value stocks, some growth stocks may offer good value. For the long-term investor willing to follow a buy and hold strategy.

Inventory level: The value of a company's unsold goods and unprocessed materials. The inventory turnover rate is the ratio of inventory to sales. Inventories accumulating faster than sales may signal price cuts and lower profits. Acceptable inventory levels may vary from one industry to another.

IPO: Initial public offering, or the company's first stock offering, usually made in a rising market, by a company issuing shares for public ownership as a means of raising capital and gaining visibility. Information about companies going public is available in a prospectus.

Long-term growth rate: The average rate at which a company's earnings grow over a period of at least three years.

Long-term investing: The strategy of buying stock in strong companies whose prices may be expected to grow over time and holding the stock through rising and falling markets. The investor relies not on a technical analysis of market behavior but on the fundamental strength of companies.

Market value: A company's share price times its total number of shares outstanding.

Mutual fund: A professionally managed portfolio of stocks in which numerous individual investors hold shares. Useful for investors who have little interest in or time for the study of company fundamentals.

Price-to-earnings (P/E) ratio: The price of stock divided by earnings per share. A measure of the amount of earnings received by the stockholder for the price of the stock. In other words, the value represented by the stock's price. Often viewed as a measure of risk and of market expectations of price movement. Trailing P/Es are based on the earnings of the previous twelve months, and future P/Es on estimates of future earnings.

Price-to-research ratio: A company's total research funding divided by the company's market value. The ratio helps the investor determine whether the stock's price is good relative to the company's level of commitment to research and development.

Return on equity: Usually, and most simply, a company's net profit divided by shareholders' equity. A broad measure of a company's profitability and efficiency.

Risk: The possibility of a permanent loss. Risk is high for short-term investors who may be forced to sell in a down market rather than waiting for prices to rebound. Different from volatility, or short-term price fluctuations.

Short interest: The number of shares held short by investors; that is, shares borrowed to be sold and later repurchased at a lower price. A measure of investor sentiment toward a stock.

Takeover: Acquisition of one company by another, rumors of which may drive up the stock price of the targeted company.

Top-down investing: Investment based on analysis of economic trends and interest rates.

Turnaround: A company in or close to bankruptcy whose potential for recovery may induce investors to purchase its stock at a low price in hopes of a later price rise.

Value stock: A stock whose price may be lower than warranted given the company's worth as determined by quantitative analysis. A stock selling at a price below its true value, with the potential to rise.

Volatility: A measure of a stock's tendency to fluctuate in price over the short term. See also RISK.

Working capital: A company's current assets minus its total liabilities. As calculated on a per share basis and compared to a stock's per share price, the single most important figure in stock picking, according to investor Benjamin Graham.

Index